THE KAEPERNICK EFFECT

THE KAEPERNICK EFFECT

Taking a Knee, Changing the World

Dave Zirin

NEW YORK
LONDON

Requests for permission to reproduce selections from this book should
be made through our website: https://thenewpress.com/contact.

Published in the United States by The New Press, New York, 2021
Distributed by Two Rivers Distribution

LIBRARY OF CONGRESS CATALOGING-IN-PUBLICATION DATA
Names: Zirin, Dave, author.
Title: The Kaepernick effect : taking a knee, changing the world Dave Zirin.
Description: New York : The New Press, 2021. | Includes index. | Summary:
"A veteran sportswriter interviews high school athletes, college athletes,
pro athletes and others involved in the nationwide movement to
'take a knee' in response to police brutality"—Provided by publisher.
Identifiers: LCCN 2021013308 | ISBN 9781620976753 (hardcover) |
ISBN 9781620976869 (ebook)
Subjects: LCSH: Sports—Social aspects—United States. |
Police brutality—United States. | Social justice—United States. |
Athletes—United States—Interviews. | Kaepernick, Colin, 1987—Influence.
Classification: LCC GV706.5 .Z569 2021 | DDC 306.4/83—dc23
LC record available at https://lccn.loc.gov/2021013308

The New Press publishes books that promote and enrich public discussion and
understanding of the issues vital to our democracy and to a more equitable world.
These books are made possible by the enthusiasm of our readers; the support
of a committed group of donors, large and small; the collaboration of our many
partners in the independent media and the not-for-profit sector; booksellers,
who often hand-sell New Press books; librarians; and above all by our authors.

www.thenewpress.com

Composition by dix!
This book was set in Fairfield LH Light

Printed in the United States of America

2   4   6   8   10   9   7   5   3   1

To Annie Zirin, sister, friend, artist,
and a true people's educator

Being brave doesn't mean not being scared. It means being scared and doing it anyway.

—A pediatrician's credo

The kneeling gesture is the spot where America comes apart, where all the post-9/11 pro-police messaging and militarism at sporting events collides with the reality of the cops and military. In no other element of our culture is there such a clear and defiant single gesture like taking a knee. Where else are we allowed the space to say we disagree with our police? Where else can we register with one gesture, dissent with the alleged ideals of this country? America is getting called out with this one gesture and they are determined to punish anyone using it.

—Howard Bryant

Contents

Preface

When this project began, "the Kaepernick Effect" referred, in my mind, to the forgotten hundreds if not thousands of young athletes who took a knee during the national anthem in protest of racism and police brutality. They were, of course, echoing the actions of former San Francisco quarterback Colin Kaepernick. These athletes and the conversations they launched were the "effect" of Kaepernick's actions. I was concerned that their protests were already being forgotten in our short-attention-span culture and wanted to tell their stories. Many of them endured on a small-town scale what Kaepernick suffered for taking a knee: death threats, ostracization, condemnation, and a whole lot more. But their stories, I feared, were being lost to the winds. I wanted to preserve them.

But now, after interviewing many of these people across the United States, I understand that the "the Kaepernick Effect" was not the result of someone else's protest, but a cause, a catalyst for something far greater. It was the warning for a future that came to pass after the police murder of George Floyd, coming on the heels of the murders of Ahmaud Arbery and

Breonna Taylor. It was the warning that people were poised and ready to fight. In the summer of 2020, we had militant marches in all fifty states in the largest, most widespread demonstrations in the history of the United States. Even with COVID-19 making its way through the population—or perhaps because COVID was spreading with its disproportionate infection and death tolls among Black and Brown families—millions were determined to have their voices heard.

"The Kaepernick Effect" and the masses of athletes who took a knee between 2016 and 2018 were the canary in the coal mine, signaling the coming struggle and also laying the groundwork for what we saw in 2020. Their efforts were aimed at starting a dialogue with their community and putting a spotlight on racist police violence. Many of the people who listened, not to mention knelt, found themselves on the streets marching for racial justice. People in power who chose to ignore them reaped the whirlwind.

"The Kaepernick Effect" was crystallized in the juxtaposition of two images. The first was Kaepernick. Then there was Minneapolis officer Derek Chauvin kneeling on the neck of George Floyd, choking him to death. For many it was like a horrific inversion of Colin Kaepernick's peaceful protest against police violence, trying to start a conversation that clearly had not been heard. "It's this sort of eerie similarity in the position that Kaepernick physically took, and the position that the officer had assumed on the neck and the head of George Floyd," Marc Lamont Hill, an activist and professor of media studies and urban education at Temple University, told ABC News. "It was almost like the flip side of it, that Kaepernick was taking a knee for justice and this man was taking a knee in ending the life of a Black man in the very fashion that Colin Kaepernick was protesting and trying to put a spotlight on."

In 2016 they didn't listen. Kaepernick and other players were called "sons of bitches" by the president; Kaepernick was forced out of his job, colluded against, and denied work. Navy SEALs had a mannequin in a Kaepernick jersey torn apart by dogs.

But two years later, the Kaepernick Effect, and the influence of his nonviolent protest, echoed loudly in the streets. Thousands of people took a knee during the George Floyd protests, Kaepernick's jersey being a popular shirt of choice for demonstrators. At different stops on demonstration routes, countless numbers would drop to one knee in a show of defiance at curfew orders, rampaging police officers, tear gas, and the idea that they should turn their backs and ignore injustice. Masses across the globe took a knee to represent not only the struggle against police violence, but broader racial inequities as well. Now people were listening. Kaepernick himself put out a single, simple message on social media: "When civility leads to death, revolting is the only logical reaction. The cries for peace will rain down, and when they do, they will land on deaf ears, because your violence has brought this resistance. We have the right to fight back!"

Even police officers attempted to appropriate the move in many cities and towns, taking a knee to show protesters that they were listening to their concerns. Some of these may have been genuine gestures of solidarity. But the media's endless reposting of the police-on-a-knee image is what people in the movement refer to as "copaganda," public relations designed to make the police look like Officer Friendly. Or as 1968 Olympian

Dr. John Carlos put it to me more succinctly, "Police posing on one knee. All that bullshit." The chant in Oakland that rang out when the police took this pose was, "We know what happens— when cops take a knee," in reference to the killer Chauvin.

In the sports world, we are also seeing the taking of the knee as a new kind of "woke branding" or "woke marketing," with players now able to do it with the approval of management and without fear of reprisal. As author Howard Bryant wrote, "Just call it for what it is: kneeling is a safe gesture now. No risk, no sanction. When it was a risk, very few people took it." Or as former NFL player Martellus Bennett put it, "Kneeling in 2020 don't hit the same."

That is true, on one level. But in many spaces in our deeply polarized country, taking the knee during the anthem invites risk, denunciation, or even violence. It really depends on which America you happen to call home.

THE KAEPERNICK EFFECT

Introduction

It was August 2016. The rather wretched San Francisco 49ers were about to play a barely noticed preseason game against the Green Bay Packers. On the sideline was then backup quarterback Colin Kaepernick. It had been a star-crossed career for Kaepernick to that point: just four years earlier, he had led the 49ers to within one play of winning the Super Bowl. Three years previously, he had led them to within one pass deflection by Seattle Seahawks cornerback Richard Sherman of making it to the championship game. And now, because of injuries and a wave of coaching changes, he was on the bench.

That was the backdrop to the game in 2016. The backdrop to the world was far more distressing. Over that summer two men, Philando Castile and Alton Sterling, were killed by police, on camera. Both were beloved members of their communities. Both were killed as if they were something less than human. Both left behind families and friends in states of abject mourning and rage. The Black Lives Matter movement was taking to the streets. WNBA players had already protested on the court that summer and were fined by their league for their activism.

These were tense times, and as the national anthem began to play, Kaepernick made the decision to walk behind his teammates and sit on the bench.

This could have gone unnoticed. The introverted Kaepernick was not exactly seeking publicity. There were no attendant press releases or exclusive interviews, stage-managed by a publicity team. But history changed when a reporter for the NFL Network, Steve Wyche, saw what was happening and asked Kaepernick why he did it. Kaepernick then uncorked a reply that would echo throughout both the sports world and the real world. He said, "I am not going to stand up to show pride in a flag for a country that oppresses Black people and people of color. To me, this is bigger than football and it would be selfish on my part to look the other way. There are bodies in the street and people getting paid leave and getting away with murder. . . . This is not something that I am going to run by anybody. I am not looking for approval. I have to stand up for people that are oppressed. . . . If they take football away, my endorsements from me, I know that I stood up for what is right."

I spoke to Wyche about pursuing this story. He said, "When Kap didn't stand, the first thing that came to mind was that over the summer, you could see he was really finding his political voice. I was wondering if Kap was sending a message by sitting. I had heard over the summer, from someone from the 49ers, that Kap was really becoming engaged with the BLM movement. I immediately had a feeling that this might be bigger than him possibly just sitting down tying his shoe or whatever. It was more of an instinct, based on the things that I heard."

Wyche had known Kaepernick since he was a senior at the

University of Nevada and was starting to get noticed by NFL scouts. "At the Senior Bowl, I went to talk to this dude. I'd never heard of him. Sweet guy, had a great conversation, met his agent there and we'd always kept in touch. I had that relationship, so I think when Kap came out to speak to me, he probably thought, 'Okay, this is someone I trust and who will take what I have to say and put it in the proper context.'"

I asked Wyche if he could possibly have imagined that Kaepernick's words and actions would fuel this kind of national outrage as well as inspiration. He said, "Nobody could've estimated it was going to be as volcanic as it's turned out to be. But I at least knew it was going to be big. I alerted our news desk and said to them before I spoke to Kap, 'If this is what I think it is, be prepared for a huge story because we have seen in this country, whenever somebody kind of "treads on the flag," people will respond.' After Kap and I did the interview, we probably spoke for five minutes, just chatting. That's when he said, 'If I lose my endorsements, if I lose my spot on the team, it's for a cause I believe in.' But I knew it was going to be a big, big story, to the point where I'm in the press room, under Levi's Stadium, with all these other reporters, just typing out this story that they've got no idea is coming."

Wyche also pointed out that Kaepernick wasn't the person most people would have predicted would become a lightning rod or any kind of a civil rights leader. In fact, if you were going to make a top ten list of athletes who would do such a thing, Kaepernick probably would not even have been a contender. "He was quiet. He kept to himself," said Wyche. "One of the knocks, by some people, against Kap was he hangs out with the guys on the bottom end of the roster. He doesn't hang out with all the stars on the team, but those are his genuine friends. As with myself and so many other people, we may not find our voice or our cause when we're twenty-three or twenty-four. We may find it later in life, and like a lot of us, he saw a whole lot of unarmed Black men getting killed by police on videotape and had enough."

After that game and the attendant outrage, Kaepernick, after discussion with former Green Beret and NFL player Nate Boyer, decided to not sit on the bench during the anthem but instead take a knee. Both Boyer and Kaepernick thought that this gesture, which would combine both dissent and a solemn respect, would calm the waters. That was, it is safe to say now, a miscalculation.

When that knee hit the ground, a debate was launched about police violence, patriotism, racism, and the history of the anthem itself. Kaepernick had also forged through his actions a link with both the Black Lives Matter movement and an often-buried history of radical athletes: people like Muhammad Ali, Tommie Smith and John Carlos, and Billie Jean King.

Kaepernick's actions also provoked something deep, ugly, and primordial in the American consciousness. They prompted a violent and highly racialized rage among a self-branded "alt-right" of racists marshaled together to support the 2016 candidacy of Donald Trump. The unrepentantly divisive and proudly bigoted Trump said on the campaign trail that Kaepernick "maybe should find another country to live in." This comment, with its "Go Back to Africa" overtones, provoked a deluge of death threats leveled at Kaepernick in city after city during that fateful 2016 season. Even with all that, Kaepernick was moved into the starting lineup and with the world breathing down his neck had a remarkable season, throwing for sixteen touchdowns and just four interceptions, while leading the NFL in yards per carry. Then came Kaepernick's exile. A league that accepts players—and owners—who have abused women, driven under the influence of alcohol, and even killed people could not stand the thought of having an avowed antiracist among "their" players, even one who engaged in community service to the extent that Kaepernick did. While taking a knee, week in, week out, Kaepernick gave away more than a million dollars to the kinds of grassroots community organizations that have trouble keeping the lights on.

The forces of NFL ownership as well as the alt-right were afraid of Kaepernick's message. They were afraid because his words were politically different from those of other athletes who had raised their voices after the police killings in the summer of 2016. His words were different because, as welcome as the outspokenness of other athletes was, they were calling for peace, whereas Kaepernick was calling for justice. Through his peaceful protest, he was proclaiming that as long as there is a gap between the values the flag purports to represent and the real world, then the fight will continue.

In this regard, Kaepernick stood in the tradition of Muhammad Ali. The great Ali did not try to "build a bridge" between the pro–Vietnam War establishment and antiwar activists. He took a side. He took a side in order to win a political fight against an unjust war.

And yet for so many frothing members of the sports media, the same sports media that had praised Ali to the heavens upon his death earlier that year, Kaepernick was an enemy. The irony of praising Ali while bashing Kaepernick was lost upon them.

Tragically, many in my profession lived up to Hunter S. Thompson's description of sportswriters as "chimps masturbating in a zoo cage."

But it was not just right-wingers, frothing sports columnists, and a racist president putting Kaepernick on blast. Liberals, people who ostensibly should have been supporting Kaepernick, also critiqued his actions. Their most common response to the anthem protest against police violence was, "I support his goal, but not his methods." This was "the line," from NFL commissioner Roger Goodell to Hall of Fame receiver Jerry Rice to quarterback Drew Brees. It was also the widely trumpeted view of conservative *New York Times* columnist David Brooks and a host of liberal Beltway pundits. Brooks, without irony, even invoked Dr. Martin Luther King Jr. to justify his position for why Kaepernick should *stop* protesting.

As for the NFL, the league exiled Kaepernick after the 2016 season, deciding that he had more value as a ghost story than as a quarterback. He was more important to franchise owners as an object lesson to haunt a new generation of players, a warning to not speak out. Despite their efforts, he has become a galvanizing spirit, inspiring a new generation of athletes to take the field of play and use it as a platform for protest. We have seen that dramatically in the aftermath of George Floyd's murder, as an unprecedented number of "jocks for justice" have stepped forward, taken a knee, demonstrated in the streets, and even gone on strike to demand justice. It's the movements, the people in the streets, that opened up the space for these athletes to be heard. It always starts in the streets. In the 1990s and 2000s, you saw athletes like NBA players Craig Hodges and Mahmoud Abdul Rauf speak out, yet in the absence of mass

struggle, they were isolated and exiled from their sports. The
year 2020 had a decidedly different flavor.

In 2020, athletes offered not only their solidarity, their
words, and their money to the protests. They put on their
marching shoes. This was such a change from 1968, when athletes were often sent to demonstrations after King was assassinated to calm things down, even in their sports uniforms. On
college campuses in the 1960s, athletes were at times used to
surround buildings that were occupied by student protesters, in
order to keep out food and supplies. Today, football players at
the Universities of Mississippi and Alabama are marching for
racial justice, not attacking the protesters. It's a bold new world.

But as we see athletes making themselves heard, we must
also remember the legion of young women and men—athletes
from all sports, and in incredibly diverse locales across the
country—taking a knee, provoking conversations, and enduring
their own backlash, without Kaepernick's financial insulation
from his years as an NFL quarterback. This book is a look at
those who took that step to kneel during the anthem, why they
did it, and how it affected their lives. It also, I believe, tells a
story about the changing politics of sports, patriotism, and the
youth who are transforming the very marrow of this country.
Their actions were a preview of the 2020 protests that rocked
the United States. They hit cities large and small and their
struggle spotlighted sports—normally a conservatizing force
in our society—as a center for fighting racial injustice. They
built a movement that put racist police brutality on trial in their
communities, placing the very nature of both the anthem and
patriotism up for debate.

In my conversations and interviews with dozens of athletes

who took a knee, certain common threads are very clear. They are bound together by a belief in racial justice. They are bound together, in almost every example, by the All-American trauma they experienced after the 2012 killing of fourteen-year-old Trayvon Martin, their generation's Emmett Till. They are bound together by the idea that they needed to take Kaepernick's effort to start a conversation and put it into action. They are bound together by the strength to withstand backlash. They braved death threats. They stood up to bigots. They were in some cases threatened with expulsion from their team. One high school football announcer in Alabama said that they should be lined up against a wall and shot. And yet they were undeterred, provoking a dialogue that this country did not want to have. They laid the foundation not only for the protests, but also for the unprecedented outpouring of athlete activism we saw in the summer of 2020. They created that space through struggle. Their actions could not be more relevant. Just because their warning fell on deaf ears does not mean it is too late to hear what they were trying to say.

1

High School

In an article called "Have We Gone Soft?" the novelist John Steinbeck wrote, "If I wanted to destroy a nation I would give it too much and I would have it on its knees, miserable, greedy and sick."

Today, young people are derided as "snowflakes," too sensitive and weak to deal with the problems that confront us in 2020. The reality is so much different. An eighteen-year-old today has been shaped by challenges that people from my generation could not hope to imagine. Her school—as a legacy of the 1999 mass shooting at Columbine High School in Littleton, Colorado—probably has metal detectors at the doors. It also has a police officer, gun at the ready, roaming the hallways. A locker-room scuffle that would have resulted in a trip to the principal's office forty years ago could now end with an arrest record. A phrase describing this process has even entered the parlance of our times, "the school-to-prison pipeline." But that's not all. High school students are being raised under the specter of ecological disaster, historic income inequality, and spiraling college tuitions. Tens of millions of them have attended school in their basements and bedrooms, under the toxic *cloud of a pandemic. Historic numbers contemplate suicide or other forms of self-harm. These are incredibly challenging times to face the world as a young adult.*

And yet, these teenagers are strong in ways that no older generation could have imagined, except perhaps those who lived through the Great Depression of the 1930s. Their very existence in these terribly challenging times is resistance, but they are doing more than existing. They are fighting back. They are answering the call and challenging the crises that envelop their lives. These high schoolers have taken part in mass walkouts for gun control, for environmental justice, and, of course, against racist police violence.

Their efforts have seeped into the world of high school sports. This is a remarkable transformation. At many high schools, sports teams are cliquish at best and at worst toxic, backward, and dismissive of anyone who stands out or is different. Coaches enforce and reinforce this ethos, with a top-down structure that prizes winning over all else and sees any semblance of free thought as a "distraction" from the ultimate goal. This is true at every level of sports—high school, college, and pro—but in high school, where the pressure to fit in is paramount, it is particularly pervasive. That is what makes it so remarkable to have seen high school athletes step out and take a knee in opposition to police violence and racial inequity.

In some cases in this chapter, you will learn of athletes who did it by themselves in the face of disapproving teammates and coaches. In other cases, the entire team took a knee, with the tacit support of coaches who believed that their mission was to develop critically thinking human beings rather than instruments for victory and the fluffing of their own egos. It's the difference between what former Baltimore Colt Joe Ehrmann refers to as "transactional versus transformational" coaching. These select few coaches didn't steer the players to satisfy their own political cravings. They only allowed the players to do what they felt was right and answer the call of the moment. This is where Colin Kaepernick becomes so important. He opened the imagination—in our hyperatomized, individualized society—to the idea that athletes could express themselves collectively as athletes and sports teams could be a platform for struggle. He created a language for this generation that athletes and politics, far from not mixing, actually have the capacity to walk hand in hand. Girls and boys, sports from football to soccer to cheer: these high school athletes exerted a different kind of leadership than in the past and were a link in the chain of a national movement.

Rodney Axson Jr., a football player at Ohio's Brunswick High School, was the first athlete in the United States, following Kaepernick, to take a knee during the anthem. Rodney saw racism and police brutality as something "that was real to me from a very young age," when he was growing up in Cleveland. His family moved to Brunswick, just outside the city, to get Rodney what they hoped would be a better education. Brunswick was a predominantly white institution where "I always had the fear of, 'Okay, if I do something that they don't like, then things are going to go sideways mighty fast.' I was a very shelled-in person throughout high school. In class, I'd talk, I was a jokester, but going out and partying every weekend was not something I felt like I could do. My fear was once people started getting drunk, I didn't know how they would respond to me. I didn't want to be put in a weird position, so I'd go home, minding

11

my business, playing *Madden*. I just trained myself into being a homebody and just being comfortable with being alone. That was my life as a Black student at Brunswick High School."

At Brunswick, Rodney was the second-string quarterback. Being a Black quarterback meant having the coaches tell his parents that he was actually the best quarterback on the team, but as Rodney remembered hearing, "'He should play corner-back, he can play safety.' With being a Black quarterback, you're always put in that box of, 'Well, you're an athlete, you're not really a quarterback. Let's have you play this position instead.' That's a story as old as football."

Rodney felt compelled to take a knee when he was in the locker room before the second game of the season against Austintown Fitch, a predominantly Black team that they faced every season. Rodney remembered two of his teammates say-ing before the game, "'We can't stand these n——ers. We're going to f—— them up!'" They were saying the N-word with the hard *r*. And so I was like, 'Whoa, wait a minute, relax.' They said, 'Oh no, don't worry, Rodney, you're one of us.' That's when I thought, 'Let's rewind. I was born Black. I am a Black man. I'm one of you guys? I'm not. I'm part of the team, but at the same time, I'm not white. I'm still a Black man in America. Why would you say that?'"

Rodney told his two other Black teammates about it and said, "'Look, I don't know what exactly I'm going to do, but I'm going to do something to fight back about this.' Because at the end of the day, I'm not going to just sit here and let that hap-pen. That really bothered me."

For Rodney, it made perfect sense that his response to the racism in his own locker room was going to be to take a knee.

The gesture was in the news because Kaepernick had started doing it, but it wasn't Kaepernick who was on his mind. "When I took the knee, I was actually thinking of my teacher Mrs. Burgess," he said. "She was talking to us about the national anthem and how the man who wrote the anthem actually owned slaves. That's when it clicked with me, in terms of what I was going to do. First, I thought I might sit on the bench. But then I thought if I did that, people could make an argument that I was being disrespectful. So I decided that I was going to take a knee and bow my head in prayer. Nobody knew that I was going to do that. The teammates that I talked to, they weren't sure what I was going to do but said, 'We're going to be with you.'"

As the stadium announcer said, "Please rise for the national anthem," Rodney stepped behind the line of coaches and "I just took a knee." The reaction was instantaneous. People in the stands started to take pictures. Parents of Rodney's teammates were snapping photos and sending them to their kids. As Rodney remembered, "They were freaking out."

When Brunswick got onto the bus after the game, everyone jumped on their phones, as teenagers tend to do, and their phones were blowing up with the photos that were sent to them of Rodney kneeling. Immediately they began posting them to the team group chat. The comments, as Rodney remembered, were, to put it mildly, not kind. "They were like, 'Why would you do that? That was so stupid. I can't believe you.' The thing was, I didn't tell anybody why I did it. I didn't defend myself in the group chat. I didn't make a big scene about it on the bus. Only the few Black players knew why I did what I did. So then I started a separate group chat with our team captains and I texted them, 'Well, here's why I did it. I didn't want to make a big deal about it and cause some huge thing. But between the three of us, in this group chat, this is why I did what I did.' Their response was more of a 'We see where you're coming from, but we think you could've handled it in a different way. We'll talk to the people that said this to you.'"

The response to Rodney is a reminder of the words of liberals to Kaepernick to, in the words of Dr. Martin Luther King's "Letter from a Birmingham Jail," "wait for a 'more convenient season.'"

That was only the initial reaction. Once back at Brunswick, it wasn't nearly as measured. Rodney's teachers were very supportive, but the students and parents were incensed. "There was a lot of negative reaction, because everybody thought I was doing it to draw attention to myself and because Kaepernick was doing it. Nobody knew the real story, except for a handful of people."

Then a death threat was sent to Rodney. It said, "Fuck Rodney. N——er. N——ers. N——ers. N——ers. Let's lynch n——ers."

"I was very scared. My family was going through a lot. I have a younger sister. It was tough for me, and it was also a thing where, when you're put into a position like that, at seventeen years old, you don't know how to respond. I don't know if I was really ready for that. I remember I was talking to my parents when I first told them about the situation. And they said, 'You have to understand that you're going to get some backlash. You got to understand the magnitude of what you just did.' Well, when I got that death threat, I did."

For a while, Rodney lived "every day in fear. The police were doing routine drive-bys through my neighborhood. Everyone was fearful. I was scared for my parents, wondering what would happen if they went out to the store and somebody recognized them. There are crazy people out there! All someone had to do was ask around and find out what elementary school my sister was going to. We've seen it time in and time out: people go to desperate measures to hurt others. That was rough: every day, fearing for the people I love."

It was a tumultuous, jarring experience, but Rodney believes that it "helped me understand the world that we live in. People say find your passion. It helped me find my passion. My passion has become that I want to be able to change this. I want to be able to find a way to make a difference. This experience drove me more. It made me hungrier to be able to make a difference. Not even for myself, but for other Black Americans put in these situations. It gave me a platform. It allowed me to be a blue-print for others to follow. I'm twenty now, but I just see life in a different light, because I understand that every day, you've got to walk around and you don't know what's going to happen. You've got to value every moment. Since then, I've gained a lot of growth, within, and a passion for wanting to make a difference, even to this day."

Something that helped Rodney push forward was learning about the heritage of Black athletes who also used their plat-form to amplify the struggles taking place in the streets. "They made history just being themselves. They were being passion-ate; they were being open. They realized they had to be differ-ent. They understood that they had to roll with the punches and be mentally strong. I watched documentaries on Muhammad

Ali, Jackie Robinson, top African American athletes that went through prejudice. I also read books about them. That was amazing. It helped me through so much."

Rodney was also inspired by Colin Kaepernick. "He was fearless; he let his voice be heard. He was a difference maker. They say quarterbacks are supposed to be the best leaders, and he showed amazing leadership. And he still stands on that same ground to this day. He hasn't changed his tune, and he moves to the beat of his own drummer. That, to me, is amazing."

After the murder of George Floyd and the subsequent mass protests happened, I reached out to Rodney. He said that when he saw the video of Floyd being killed, "it wasn't a reaction of disbelief. This is America and we've seen this before. But it still stings. I was extremely saddened and hurt, especially with seeing how some people are still trying to take the side of the police officer. It was just unbelievably brutal, watching the video, and watching that man scream for his life. It brought me to tears."

As for the militant demonstrations that followed, Rodney said, "I'm going to be completely honest: I love it. I'm happy with the protests. Don't get me wrong, there's a couple of things where they're just doing the extreme looting, and I want to say, 'Wait a minute, that's not helping the cause.' At the same time, I understand the looting because after years and years of tolerating things, you reach a breaking point. With the riots and the protests, I am completely behind them. I love them because it's getting world coverage. They're putting the government in a position where I hope at some point they are going to have to make some kind of changes."

I asked Rodney if he believes his actions helped lay the

groundwork for what we are seeing. He said, "I'll put it like this: I feel like we helped lay the groundwork for this era because I think a lot of people wanted to be ignorant to the fact that racism and police brutality are something in the present. Too many people think it is something of the past. Once myself and others around the nation took a knee, it kind of forced people into having the conversation. Now it's forcing people into realizing, 'Oh, this stuff is really happening.' I think it's so crazy because people think, 'That was so long ago when things were bad,' and it really wasn't. I was watching an interview with Kareem Abdul-Jabbar, and he talked about remembering when Emmett Till was murdered. That happened when he was eight years old. It's not ancient history!"

As for whether the protests make him feel vindicated for his highly criticized actions, Rodney said, "Absolutely! Absolutely, because I feel like it's now reached a point where a lot of people realize why we did it. To me it's a thing where, now if you're saying you don't understand it, you just want to be blind to the truth. I feel like I'm vindicated because it's blossomed into something beyond America. People are taking a knee all over the world. I loved that in the United Kingdom they took down a statue of a slave trader and threw it into the water. That just shows that this is real. You guys have to sit here and swallow your words of saying racism isn't real and we're overreacting and this stuff doesn't happen anymore. It *is* happening and it's happening in front of you, to where you can't ignore it. That's why I do feel a sense of vindication."

Often when you have conscientious, serious young people willing to take risks in order to fight racism, a supportive adult is not too far in the background. April Parkerson is a mom in Beaumont, Texas, a city of 120,000 people. Beaumont sits in one of the reddest parts of the state. "Let me kind of put things into perspective for you," said April. "I don't know if you've ever heard of Vidor, Texas, but it's about ten miles away from us, and is still considered a 'sundown town'. Not a lot has changed in the last fifty years." For those unfamiliar with the term, "sundown towns" are all-white communities that would respond with intimidation and violence—either by police or vigilantes—to any people of color or "undesirables" caught driving or working after sundown.

April's son Jaelun was one of those kids who was a born athlete, climbing over anything and everything in the house. "And just to save furniture, we decided to put him into something organized to channel a lot of that energy." That meant football. That meant, at age eleven, joining the Beaumont Bulls. That also put Jaelun in a position, along with his team, to take a knee in 2016.

April said, "I've always been pretty open and honest with my kids. Trying to let them know what goes on in the world and what you need to be prepared for. The summer before that football season started, there were the killings of Philando Castile and Alton Sterling. The Alton Sterling killing happened about three hours away from us and we visited the memorial a couple of months after it happened. Seeing those things play out live, because these days, everything's on Facebook or Instagram Live, really sparked something in our kids, and they wanted to know what could we do, how could we make a difference, and asking, 'Can we even make a difference?' They were angry and confused, hurt, and they just needed a creative way to vent some of that: channel that energy and do something positive."

April said that the coach, Rah-Rah Barber, was supportive when he heard that the kids were going to kneel. But he was also apprehensive "because, as most of us adults were aware, he knew the backlash that those kids would face."

It started with the kids convincing the parents and then their coach that they understood the reasoning behind their actions. The next step was the coach talking to all the parents without the kids being present. Then the parents were in favor of taking this step.

The first game saw the entire team on one knee, their hands on each other's shoulders. They then took the field, beating the Pasadena Panthers 27–0.

The reaction started well enough, according to April. "In the very beginning, I would say the majority of the black community and progressive community was behind our boys and very supportive, especially the publicity that they received. But it kind of projected them into the national spotlight and I think some of the parents weren't ready for that, and most likely, our board of directors and the league, as a whole wasn't ready. That, I believe, is what made the board members, the league, and some of the parents rethink allowing the protests to continue, or allowing their children to take part in it. Because once the kids hit the national news, that's when we started receiving death threats and a lot of the threats were from local people. I can remember several of them very vividly. These were grandparents threatening our children. These were adults."

April wasn't surprised by the threats. "Just more disappointed, and it really made our boys know that they were doing the right thing. It proved that it was necessary." As the threats rolled in, events started to move very quickly.

"What happened next was our board of directors told us that we were no longer allowed to protest and if we continued to protest, they would kick our sons off the team." The boys weren't removed at first, but Coach Barber was "suspended for not following league protocol."

Then, in the aftermath of Coach Barber's removal, the entire team was disbanded for their actions. "You know, we never expected that we would be forced to leave the Beaumont Bulls. With it being an all-Black league, we thought we'd have the support needed to continue and grow from this. It just didn't happen anything like that. Once they cancelled our season, a few of us got together and decided to form a new league, and that's what we did. We got together, we got our 501(c)3, non-profit status, IRS, and all the proper channels we needed to be considered a nonprofit."

These families then received funding from the Malcolm Jenkins Foundation—a group run by the then Philadelphia Eagles pro bowler—who purchased $20,000 worth of equipment so they could start their new league. Other NFL players contributed as well. "It made us happy. It made us very grateful and it really showed the boys, hey, when you're doing something right, positive things will come. Yes, there's a lot of negativity, a lot of backlash—these kids went through a lot, but it paid off in the long run. Three years later now, we've attracted over 250 kids to our organization and it's grown tremendously. We're a bunch of like-minded individuals. We do much more than just football and cheer. We help tutor these kids and we provide them with food during the summer. We're really more of a community, a family."

They are now known as the Southeast Texas Oilers in a brand-new league with five teams.

The knowledge that Jaelun has taken from the experience, according to April, was "adults are not always right. And that you can't always trust them, that's one of the hard lessons he's learned. Sometimes, if you know you're doing the right thing and an adult is telling you to stop, continue doing what you're doing. There's always a price to pay for doing the right thing, as sad as that sounds."

Jaelun also learned that protest is necessary to bring out the best in people. "This is something that Jaelun said, time and time again, to anybody he's talked to. Black, white, Hispanic, it doesn't matter. We're all the same inside. He said it just takes some of us a little bit longer to realize that we're all the same. We all have the same wants and needs, goals and dreams. We all have to work, eat, and provide for our families. We should all be able to do that without having a target on our back."

The decision to fight back impressed upon everyone that being an antiracist requires vigilance. "Ahmaud Arbery was killed for jogging. That really upset my kids all over again. Our kids are cute and they're not really seen as threatening, but what happens when our babies turn seventeen, eighteen, twenty-one, whatever? They're not seen as those cute little boys anymore. Now they're seen as, 'Oh no the scary Black man.' What can we do to change that? Or change people's perception. We always thought that racism would die with the older generation; however, there are so many young people that are fueled by so much hatred. The resurgence of hate that we've seen, none of us really expected it to be this way. We bought a home about two years ago and started going through the neighborhood. One of the neighbors, two streets back, had an Aryan Brotherhood flag, along with his Confederate flag, along with his Trump flag."

As for April, she wants it known that "police brutality is still an issue. I'm white. Jaelun is biracial. White privilege is real and we need to do our job at changing as much as we can, because we've got to really work together in order to make this work. It's going to take us using our privilege to piss a few people off to get things done."

People know Richard Johnson II as RJ. He was one of the students who, as a senior, took a knee at Capital Christian Academy, in Prince George's County, Maryland, a majority Black suburb that borders Washington, DC. PG County, as it is known, is a place of both affluence and poverty. The population is 65 percent Black, while the police force is only 43 percent Black. Its police department is notorious for racism, both on the streets and inside the force itself, in regard to its promotional practice toward Black officers.

RJ made his feelings clear about living in a community where the threat posed by police is very real. "As a Black man, I do feel that I have a certain connection to each and every case of police violence that involves another Black man," he said. "I feel like I look at it from a personal perspective, where I have a relationship with the person who was harmed. I don't physically feel what they've experienced, but I feel it anyways. I am aware of it."

RJ was a leader on a team that made national news when they decided collectively, with the blessing of their coach, to take a knee. "The original inspiration was Colin Kaepernick," he said. "We wanted to bring awareness to the issue and this was a way to do it. We said to each other, 'We're not going to act like this isn't going on. This is a problem that needs to be solved.'"

That the players at CCA did it as a team negated any feelings of isolation or fear experienced by so many who have taken that step. When a team does it as one, it acts as a protective force field: they are all in it together. "I knew throughout the entire time that I took a knee that I had each and every one of my brothers right beside me. We were received pretty well by the school. They were just like, 'The football team is taking a knee to bring awareness to police brutality.' That is exactly what we wanted to happen: to bring awareness to our community."

While they were received well at home games, there were incidents on the road. One time in particular, the team bus pulled into a gas station in a rural, predominantly white town, and "words were exchanged" with a group of people who, disturbingly, had followed the bus from the football field to the gas station. "I was a captain at the time and I just told everyone to sit down and shut up, pretty much, just don't say anything. Put the windows up. Just had to get everyone under control, just to make sure that we weren't reacting to them. Just trying to get back to school safely because you never know."

The process of leading a team that was attempting to spread this message was an unforgettable experience for RJ. "I definitely learned some leadership skills," he said. "I definitely learned organizational skills making sure that everybody was comfortable and on board. I made the rule as one of the captains that if anybody wasn't down, if there was one person that didn't want to take a knee, then we weren't taking a knee. It would either be the whole team or nobody. There was a little bit of debate and discussion from a couple of freshmen that wanted to know a little bit more. But all we had to do was pull them to the side and let them know. I just told them to ask us whatever questions they had and we answered them. It's a simple concept of spreading awareness. Just letting everybody know that this issue is not something that we're going to ignore. It's a problem we're going to be a part of solving, somehow. Overall, I'm just glad that I had a team that was genuinely with me and on board with everything that followed. It made everything a lot easier and we definitely became closer as brothers. I've never been on another football team that I've been closer with than that team."

RJ said of his coach, Cornell Wade, "That's a great coach! He's a great person and helped me get to where I am right now."

Coach Cornell Wade grew up in Prince George's County. He said, "Capital Christian is small. It has some very good things about it. Close-knit. It is really open. They were really open to the idea we had, in regard to taking a knee and seeing the guys take a stand for what they believe in."

Coach Wade remembered that the entire team took a knee after the team met on their own to debate it out. Then the senior captains came to him with the idea.

"They had a players-only meeting before they spoke with me. So by the time we spoke, the team was already united and it was a conversation in regard to making sure they understood the deeper purpose: what the process would look like and the backlash that they might face. We just wanted to make sure our young men knew what the statement was for, the deeper meaning behind it, and the consequences for their actions."

The team told Coach Wade that they felt compelled to do it because of their own experiences with police violence. "The majority of them had already experienced it in their lives. Four or five guys spoke about different issues that they'd had with police. We had one young man who was actually on probation at the time, and he shared his very rich experience with the courts and the legal system. But I would say, all together, that would be the reason: police brutality and really wanting to make a statement around it."

Coach Wade said he felt no nervousness about doing it. "If anything, I felt pride. This is a group of young men who had made a decision, on their own, to do something that I never thought a high school football team would do. For me, the biggest takeaway was that there's some level of hope for the next generation, if I can just be totally honest with you. I'm twenty-eight and I see a huge difference in their upbringing and mine and the values that are instilled in today's young people."

I asked Coach Wade if, when he was coming up as a football player, he could have imagined that the football field would be a place of dissent or a place of resistance. Coach Wade laughs deeply. "No. No, sir, I could not. I had never seen it before!"

Coach Wade thinks the potential for football to be this kind of force is something that has always existed in the sport. "It's a testament to the power of the game. I grew up in Bladensburg [in Prince George's County]. We had teammates who were African. We had teammates who had Hispanic heritage. We had African American teammates. We had Caucasian teammates. Football is a sport that really promotes working together and getting past personal differences. I don't want to give football too much credit, but I believe that the emergence of a gentleman like Kaepernick really only happens in football. I think football is a sport that promotes that type of bravado to just say what you need to say."

As for Colin Kaepernick, Coach Wade sees someone who has been both a role model and a martyr. "He sacrificed his career for a greater good, a greater purpose, so I am a huge fan of Colin Kaepernick. Some of the quarterbacks who have jobs right now, it's ridiculous he's not out there. I mean, he got to a Super Bowl before all this stuff happened. Then you've got quarterbacks who throw thirty picks a year who are still playing."

Coach Wade now runs the Royalty Institute, a private high school centered on the education of young men of color. He was partially inspired to get this off the ground by being at Capital Christian in 2018 and being part of this team that took a knee. "We have twenty young men. It somewhat stems from this conversation around Kaepernick and being more proactive in the development of young men of color and the lives of people of color in this country. It's been going phenomenally. The community supports us. We've gotten a bunch of athletes who have really wanted to change the way they've gone about things."

The taking of the knee was transformative not only for the young people but for Coach Wade himself.

Camden, New Jersey, is not an easy place to survive. It is the poorest city in the United States. Before wholescale police reform took place, it was statistically the most dangerous city in the United States, with a murder rate on par with Honduras's. Camden is a place where the life expectancy is more than a decade shorter than in the rest of the state; it's also a place where the high school football team decided that it would be a symbol of hope and resistance.

Preston Brown was the coach at Woodrow Wilson High School, where he and his team decided to take a knee. Coach Brown did not have an easy childhood. "Growing up in Camden, in the early nineties, for a lot of my childhood was hard as nails. I've seen just about anything that you can imagine. Drug deals, drug busts, shoot-outs, police rundowns. I moved quite frequently. My mother had struggles with addiction. She was in a really bad car accident when I was a young kid that fractured both her hips and her kneecaps. She was in a wheelchair for about nineteen months. They told her at one point that she'd never walk again. But she got out of that chair."

Coach Brown's personal decision to not stand for the anthem predates Kaepernick. "For me it's something I've been doing for a very long time in my life. My Haitian grandmother had explained to me, when I was a small kid, how the national anthem didn't necessarily apply to people who looked like her and me. Then I used to get sent to the principal's office in fifth and sixth grade, because I refused to recite the Pledge of Allegiance or stand for the national anthem. When I was in the choir, I refused to sing the national anthem at the opening of the Christmas play. For a month, my punishment was I had to walk home for lunchtime. I couldn't have lunch with my classmates. When Kaepernick did it, I was like, wow, I've been doing this since I was eleven years old."

Brown was impressed with Kaepernick because "he's worth millions of dollars, but he's fighting oppression for people like me and the kids that I see each and every day. I buried three former players last year. Since I've been coaching, I believe it's been five total."

Coach Brown saw kneeling as a way to make a statement against the injustice that marks daily life in Camden. He gathered his team and said, "'At tomorrow's game, I'm going to kneel, and you guys are free to make your own choices and own decisions, but this is the reason why I'm doing it.' The one thing I tried to get across to many, many people is that it has absolutely zero to do with disrespecting anyone of any kind. It was because there are things that some kids endure in the city of Camden that most kids would never know or even fathom to think possible." Brown's team was ready to do it and they knelt with their coach.

The response from the community was "half and half. There were a lot of folks that were calling me names, saying I should leave the country," he said. "People sent threats or whatever. Not that I ever was afraid or scared. It didn't even faze me, not one bit. But the kids saw the reaction of people and it taught them something very important. You can play ball really well. People will come and love you for that. But because you think differently about outside issues that affect you in a way that makes life seem unequal, those same people will call you 'n——ers.' They will send your coach messages and call you a coon and say all kinds of names. I still got those messages too. I saved them. But they also saw the support. There was an overwhelming number of letters coming in from across the world once an article about what we did came out in the BBC. There was an abundance of letters from folks across Europe, sending us notes saying, 'Way to stand up, young people!' There was a large amount of that, too. It's like anything else. Star quarterback shows up, he plays great in one game, 'We love you, we love you.' You stink it up the next week, it's like, 'Get rid of him.'"

Coach Brown is one of the few coaches who took leadership on this issue. The default position of most coaches was to discourage their players who felt the need to act. I asked him why that was the case and he said, "I think a lot of people don't like controversy. The same people would show up to a private bar or party and voice their opinions as much as they want. But in a public forum, they would stay reserved to maintain their public perception. There were countless people that sent messages to me saying, 'I admire your courage. I admire what you're doing and I believe in the fight that you're fighting, I just can't say it publicly because of my job. Or because people in my family would disagree with me and I don't want to get disowned.'"

I asked Coach Brown if he had any regrets to share about what went down. He said, not surprisingly, "No, I have absolutely zero regrets about anything. I always tell people, the one thing that you will get from Preston Brown, you will know exactly where I stand as a man. Right, wrong, indifferent, agree to disagree, whatever you want to call it amongst people, but you know exactly where I stand and I'm always going to stand on the line and protect my people. When I say 'my people,' that's not just a Black thing. It's the people that I interact with. The people that I call family: my friends, my loved ones, my network of people who are from all walks of life and various backgrounds."

Coach Brown also has something to say, big picture, about the confluence of sports and patriotism, which is such a feature of the post-9/11 world. "When I was growing up in middle school and playing youth football, I never remember a single game where they played the national anthem. Not one. When I was in college at Tulane, we'd be in the locker room. Now I'm at youth games for five- and six-year-olds and they're making loud announcements, saying everyone needs to stand up. I'm thinking, 'Why are they making such a huge deal about it?' They're trying to intertwine sports and patriotism and they are not synonymous."

The Detroit metro area is defined by savage inequalities. The city is 78 percent Black, with 36 percent living below the poverty line. (Those numbers come from 2019, before the ravages of COVID could be considered.) Surrounding the city are some of the wealthiest suburbs in the United States. These two worlds collided in a football game when Denby High School from Detroit tried to bring their reality into a setting that was not trying to hear what they had to say.

Coach Bob Burg is an assistant coach at Denby. He wears a lot of hats—special teams, trainer, mentor—because at Denby, you make do with what you have. "We've got great athletes. Academically we're very sound. The thing is we're from a very poor area of Detroit. We have to be fathers, grandfathers . . . we're everything that we need to be to help the kids."

The challenges at Denby are extreme. Number one, according to Coach Burg, is "the safety of kids when they leave. After practice, we do everything we can, but you don't want them going down the wrong street."

Denby made it to the state semifinal game against Almont, a predominantly white school, and the game was held at a neutral field, also in a predominantly white suburb. As the players took a knee before the game, they were showered with invective and even trash, thrown by the Almont fans in the stands. That set the tone for the even greater ugliness to come. As Coach Burg remembered, "Our kids are great kids, but they were treated like nothing I've ever seen, sir. It was a bad, bad day. I only wish that everybody thought about giving each kid the same amount of love, no matter what color their skin is. I'm a sixty-one-year-old coach with thirty-seven years in the game, and I don't have any answers for what went on."

It started with the people in the stands. "I'm not going to say they were all Almont people. It was supposed to be a neutral site. But Almont draws a lot more fans than we do. Most of our kids' parents aren't even involved in their lives. Some grandparents and relatives got out there, but Almont was five-thousand-deep with their fans. From the opening kick, things were being said in the stands. The message was 'You don't belong here.'"

In other words, due to the tenor of the crowd, even if the Denby players hadn't taken a knee, there was trouble brewing. It was so ugly that Denby supporters had to leave the bleachers and stand on the sideline with the Denby team so they would feel safe.

What happened after the game, Coach Burg said, "I'll never forget. It's heartbreaking, really. Racism is alive in this country. I don't know, I wish I had an answer. I usually have an answer for everything, but I can't understand it all. It was the crowd and it was the refs. Call after call went against Denby on the road to defeat. Then the mood turned very ugly on the field and the game was just stopped by the officials with four minutes left, handing Almont the victory.

"We would've loved to congratulate Almont after the game

and said, 'Congratulations, go on, win the state championship,' because that was our opponent and we respect our opponents, win or lose. But we weren't even given the opportunity to shake hands."

After the game was called, the Denby players were instead pinned into the corner of the end zone as Almont swarmed the field. There they were bumped and jostled by the Almont band. Punches were thrown and the melee went viral.

Coach Burg is now trying to start fresh with his team and be treated fairly by opponents and referees alike, especially when they are outside the Detroit city limits. "I'd love nothing more than to talk to Mr. Kaepernick and ask him what we can do this year so we aren't singled out. We want the memory of what happened to go away, sir. People won't let it go away. We want to leave and start fresh and win a state championship. Let's play football. Let's get out there. Let's get the great grades and grow. . . . I'm lost. We have so much that's negative in the surrounding area of our school. There are murders; there's somebody killed every week. These kids are so tough and resilient; they move on. . . . It's just sad. We would've liked to have a level playing field. . . . I don't know, I'm so frustrated. You know everybody has rights. I can't come forward and say, 'Gentlemen, do not take a knee; no more.' This is not what it's about. These kids are athletes. Everybody has freedom of speech."

Isaiah Pollack was one of the Denby players who took a knee against Almont. He did so because of "the injustice around our city and around America, period."

He knew it could be a long game, not only from the crowd reaction but from the ways that "the white cap" (the crew leader of the referees) was looking at them as they took a knee.

Here is Isaiah's description of the hell that broke loose after the game: "The band is leaving the stadium. Everybody knows the band is supposed to stay where they're at and the football players are supposed to leave the field first. The band's walking in front of us while we're trying to leave, and they're basically slamming their instruments against us and doing extra, you know what I'm saying? We're already pissed off, because we knew we got cheated in the game. It just got out of hand."

Describing the scene, Isaiah said, "You had to be there, really. You had to see it. But I can explain it to you too. To see the hatred and just plain racism to the fullest, that's what it was. It was nothing else. Plain racism. We didn't expect a backlash for taking a knee, because we felt like we didn't do anything wrong. At the end of the game, when the parents and others in the stadium started spitting at us and doing other stuff like that, we were already mad because, like I said before, we were getting cheated."

Isaiah said that he has "no regrets at all about taking a knee, because it's what we stood for, we still stand for. Things going on now, with the George Floyd incident, this is the main reason why we take a knee and why we don't put our right hand over our heart, because we feel that something's got to change for us to feel proud of being Americans. I've seen police brutality too many times to remember. I've seen stuff like that in my hood and all over Detroit. It's not a onetime thing; I've seen it multiple times. There's nothing fake about that. These incidents happen."

James A. Garfield High School in Seattle is a place where you can feel the history thrum throughout the hallways. Quincy

Jones and Jimi Hendrix were students here. Dr. Martin Luther King Jr. spoke on the grounds. It's always been a fulcrum of debate, culture, and big-time high school sports. It makes sense that the first place in the country that saw entire teams take a knee was at Garfield. But it wasn't all garlands and glory.

Their football coach at the time, Joey Thomas, was at the heart of what went down. He's now coaching in Florida, and the first thing he said when we spoke was, "I saw in your email that you wanted to talk about Garfield High School and the process by which the team took a knee. What part of the process do you want to talk about? Do you want to talk about the part where they tried to fire me? The part where they tried to take my job away? The part where I finally resigned? We were the only school that unanimously did this. This came with a bunch of death threats and a whole bunch of other poo-poo."

I did in fact want to hear all the poo-poo. To understand what happened, you need to start by understanding that Garfield is a school deeply tied to Coach Thomas's life. He grew up in Seattle in the city's Central District, the same neighborhood where Garfield resides. "For me, that is home. I played at the University of Washington, later transferred to Montana State, where I was an All-American, and I went on to play five years in the NFL. I came home after I retired due to injury and I went straight into teaching and learning. Yes, we won games, and yes, that's phenomenal, but it's about empowering the lives of the youths. Our greatest message to them is, 'You are the future, but we have to grow you, nurture you, and develop you mentally, so when you leave this program, you can have a good foundation.' School's put in place not to educate. It's to make you comply. So our job was to push back against that, educate kids and also listen to them. The thing that's really fascinating is that kids are so much smarter than what we give them credit for, and if you actually listen to them and allow them to talk through their issues, problems, or their perspective . . . oh my gosh, the things you'll learn."

Coach Thomas's thoughts about policing were formed by his own life in the Central District of the city. "When you grow up and you're five or six, hey, the police are going to give you candy. You run to the police when things are bad, 'Hey, Officer, I need some help, this is happening.' I would probably say, I think that wore off around fifth grade. There's not one incident, but I think at that point, you're no longer naive that everything's okay. The sky is blue, the grass is green, the police are the police. This is how life is."

The process that brought the football team to taking a knee and making national headlines started with one player who came up to Coach Thomas the day before a game and said, "Coach, this Kaepernick thing is crazy. Man, let's take a knee."

Coach Thomas nixed that, saying that the team needed to have a conversation before they took such a step. Then another player during the next week asked about Kaepernick, and that led to the squad having a dialogue about what was happening. "We talked it out: What was he doing? Why was he doing it? What does that mean to them? You know, a lot of kids said, 'Hey, man, I don't quite understand it.' So we talked about the national anthem's third verse and what that third verse really means. I had them read it out loud and asked them, 'You tell me what it means,' because young men always ask, 'What do you think?' My job is to help them become critical thinkers, not think for them. I always said, 'What do you think? Let's read

it out loud until you have a greater understanding.' Each individual came to the belief that, hey, when they're talking about
these liberties and justice, they're not speaking about me."

The third verse, never sung before sporting events, reads in
part:

> No refuge could save the hireling and slave
> From the terror of flight or the gloom of the grave,
> And the star-spangled banner in triumph doth wave
> O'er the land of the free and the home of the brave.

This was in reference to the enslaved people who escaped
bondage and joined the British Army in the War of 1812 because of promises of freedom. The writer of the anthem, Fran-
cis Scott Key, was taking triumphant joy in the deaths of the
enslaved. His joy may have been influenced by the fact that
Key was himself a slaveholder. In the last two lines, Key takes a
wrecking ball to irony by saying that the escaped enslaved people killed on the battlefield while fighting for their liberation is
further proof of the glory of the "land of the free and the home
of the brave." As journalist Jon Schwarz wrote, "Maybe it's all
ancient, meaningless history. Or maybe it's not, and Kaepernick
is right, and we really need a new national anthem."

The Garfield players, armed with this history, were ready to
take that knee. I asked Coach Thomas if he was nervous before
they did it. He said, "No, I wasn't, because, to be honest, I didn't
understand the gravity of the situation. I don't think anyone understood what lay ahead or what would come from this. I saw
it as an educational opportunity to stand by and support these
young men as they grow and find themselves. I didn't think it

was a big deal. The kids felt like doing something righteous, and what type of educator would I be if I didn't support that? They weren't hurting anyone. It wasn't damaging anything. It wasn't disrespectful. It wasn't harmful. I didn't see the political backlash or the fallout that lay ahead. I just saw that these kids strongly believe this. I'm going to support them. This is what it is. If I'm wrong, then I'm wrong, but I'm supporting my kids."

The backlash against Garfield detonated and it came from all corners: "We had death threats. The kids were told that they were never going to get into college. People said they would do everything they could to make sure they wouldn't get in through admissions. I was called every name in the book. And my tires were slashed at my house. This is my home. My wife and kids are there. My residence! I had to move. I had to move residences because people knew where I lived."

The school district, feeling the backlash, wanted Garfield football to stop kneeling. They blamed Coach Thomas, and he paid for it with his job. First they charged him with a bogus recruiting violation, of which he was quickly cleared, and then they tried to change his job title. Eventually, the harassment became too much and he left the school to which he had dedicated so much of his life. "They were definitely trying to force me out, one way or the other," he said. Now Joey Thomas is far from the place he called home, working at Florida Atlantic University. "Obviously the stance we took was unpopular. Do I think it's hurt me professionally? Without question. Was I hesitant to take this interview? Without question. But right is right and wrong is wrong. Am I still concerned about backlash at this point? Yeah, of course I am, because I already experienced it. It's been shown to me what can happen."

Coach Thomas said of his players, "Everybody's proud they did it because we understand in hindsight that we were part of history, but it's very important for people to understand we didn't know it was going to be like this. We didn't plan on it being like this. We're just Garfield. We're just a high school in Seattle, Washington, standing for what we believed in. Before we knew it, we were in *USA Today*, the *LA Times*, *Time* magazine. . . . Who saw that coming? We were interviewed for two or three documentaries. No one anticipated that. The misconception was that we wanted the attention. Man, we didn't ask for any of that. I sure didn't ask to be catapulted to the front seat. But I think it was a comfortable narrative for people to push. Here's the key: it was a student-led thing, but it was convenient for the powers that be to say it was coach-led because then they're able to give it a face. But when it's student-led, you can't do that. And as a coach, you can't do anything but support your kids. So I think there was such a conscious effort to deface what was going on and put a spin on it. In the end, that's what cost me. But hey, I would do it again. I'm always going to fight for what I believe in, but pushing what I believe was never the goal. The intention was to show these young men that they have a voice, that they are important, that they matter."

Being attacked from all corners also brought the team and the school together. "Even though we did get support from everybody in our community, there was a long period of time when we were lonely and we were by ourselves," said Coach Thomas. "I think it's always easier when people see other people supporting, they jump on the bandwagon. But there were some lonely days, there were some lonely weeks, and there were some lonely nights. Before it was popular to kneel with Kap, we were there. And believe me: it was quite unpopular."

Jelani Howard was part of that team. Seeing the gentrification taking place throughout Seattle was something that changed him when he was growing up: the creation of wealthy neighborhoods where he was clearly not wanted. Like so many young people in what we could call "Generation Trayvon," he hurtled toward becoming a changemaker when Trayvon Martin was murdered by George Zimmerman. "When Trayvon Martin was killed, that's when I started realizing, 'Oh, this is actually real.' Before that, I never thought of police brutality or anything like that, but when that happened, that's when I really opened my eyes."

Jelani has his own narrative about how Garfield made their small piece of history. "Well, it first all started because Coach Thomas used to have these talks with us in the summer about what's going on in the world, before we'd even go to practice or before we'd watch film. Trump was running for office and we were talking about what was going on. Then, during preseason, Kaepernick took a knee, and after that game, we had a talk about why he did it. That just led us on to other conversations. We even started talking about how other verses of the national anthem talked about killing slaves—we went into depth about that. It started with conversations about why we were taking a knee and connecting it to what's going on in the world."

After they took a knee, Kaepernick spoke about the Garfield actions to the *Seattle Times*, saying, "We have a younger generation that sees these issues and want to be able to correct them. I think that's amazing. I think it shows the strength, the character, and the courage of our youth. Ultimately, they're going to be needed to help make this change."

What made Garfield exceptional—and what caught Kaepernick's attention—was that, as Jelani remembered, "It was the whole team. Even the managers and even the cheerleaders started taking a knee." It also made national news, but that meant a national backlash: "At first, we had a Facebook picture of our entire team," he said. "People would comment on it saying nasty or disrespectful things. Then there was the one morning where our head coach didn't show up and everybody was just confused. He finally got there like an hour late and he told us that somebody had slashed his tires. That's when everybody knew, wow, this is real. People are really mad about us doing this. They know where he lives and decided to slash his tires. That really opened my eyes."

As for regrets, Jelani said, "I have none. It's something that I'll always be able to tell my kids. I did something that I will always remember, because it showed me that if you want to stand up for something, just go do it. Nobody thought that fifteen-, sixteen-, seventeen-year-old kids would be able to help lead a movement. I had the opportunity to be in *Time* magazine, something that really makes me proud. I have no regrets because we had a motivation. We as a team wanted to see social equality for everybody because we live in a society where, if you're a person of color, you're already on the back burner. If there's a Black person and a white person that has the same degree, same everything, that white person will make more than that Black person, just off of race. That just doesn't sit right with me. I want to be able to change that for the next generation, instead of them having to go through that."

Jelani also has advice for others thinking about stepping forward and speaking out. "If there's anybody that feels like they can make a change in the world or in their community, and they don't feel like they have the voice to do it, or don't feel comfortable doing it, I feel like they should still try. First of all, the experience is good, to just see everything that you're doing. Second of all, you have a voice and you should use it and you shouldn't be scared of what people will say or what will happen, because there's people that went before us, that went through harsh things, way worse things than we're going through right now, and still decided to use their voice to make a change in this world. If they can do it, I feel like anybody can do it. You shouldn't let people or a group of people stop you or scare you from doing that."

Once the football team took a knee, it spread to other sports at the school. Janelle Gary was part of the softball team at Garfield High School that took a knee. She played on a select team growing up, and once an umpire made a snide remark about her being one of the few Black girls on the field. She was only ten years old at the time. "That is something I'll never forget," she said.

As for police violence, this was something that Janelle was always aware of. But it wasn't until social media highlighted the killing of Trayvon Martin and other Black people who've been affected by racial violence and police brutality that it hit home. "I knew it was there, but now actually watching the videos myself, it just brought it more into reality for me."

Janelle and her team at Garfield decided to also protest during the anthem because "our football squad at Garfield started taking a knee and they got a lot of backlash, especially the football coach. People were threatening the school and him and his children. We wanted to stand up by taking a knee." The stage was set for the team to act.

"My team was already the most diverse that made it to state," she said. "Being an inner-city school, we definitely had the most people of color. A lot of people thought it was a fluke that we made it to state, and we just wanted to show that girls from a diverse school could come together and win. We wanted to show solidarity, not only with Colin Kaepernick and everyone protesting in America, but also to support our football team and show that Garfield believes in this, together."

They also wanted to bring what is unique about Garfield, a high school whose students and faculty are often on the front lines of social justice movements in the Seattle area. "Even at our school, like, for assemblies, our principal gives us the option of whether we want to stand or sit for the national anthem. We just wanted to bring to state that part of Garfield."

The team was united in wanting to take a knee. They also knew, based upon what happened to the football team, that backlash was a probability. Therefore, it wasn't a surprise when they took their knee and a lady yelled from the stands, "Shame on you, Garfield!"

"After that, a lot of teams were really rude to us," Janelle said. "I remember us getting ready and warming up, and then during the game, one parent was antagonizing us and making comments every time we went up to bat. That was a lot for us to take in, being the most diverse team there and then having parents from the stands yell things at you. Even when we were done with the game, when it was our lunch break, a bunch of parents from other schools found us and went out of their way to keep on yelling, 'Shame on you, Garfield. Shame on you!' No one asked why we were doing it or anything like that. They just came and attacked us. It was really hard, at that age, because we were very emotional. We didn't think that people would attack kids like that, as adults."

If Janelle could do it all over again, "even with the backlash," she would do it. "A lot of times in general, when it comes to protesting, people hear the backlash. People say negative things to try to scare you on purpose, but if you're able to persevere through that—like in the days of the civil rights movement—I feel like you're going to see more change. Nowadays, they are purposefully trying to stop a movement, because they know how big it can become. I would definitely want to continue and speak out about why we were doing it, just to have a better opportunity to get the message out there and get people to understand."

Two years after taking a knee, the team won the state championship. "I think that was our sweet revenge. I did appreciate the outcome, being the first inner-city school to win state, period, because most of the time it is the private schools that win or schools from the north end of the city."

Janelle also helped start an organization, New Generation, "after the death of Charleena Lyles, a Seattle Public Schools mother, who was shot and killed by the police." New Generation organized demonstrations and raised money for Lyles's family. They also worked closely with NFL player and then Seattle Seahawk Michael Bennett to make sure that Charleena Lyles's name would not be forgotten. According to Janelle, "The purpose of this group is to fight for issues that matter to young people and see that they don't get swept under the rug. People don't really understand the injustices that happen in the system, and so it's really important that we, as young people, bring that to light and let people in our community know what's going on. Even with Charleena Lyles, her family was part of Seattle Public Schools, but a lot of people in Seattle didn't even know about her story. That in itself was huge for us—people in our own community didn't even know about her killing. It's not okay that a woman lost her life—not even only her life; she was pregnant—and she got shot in front of her other three kids. Getting people to know her story, to make sure she wasn't forgotten, is what made me passionate about being an activist and wanting to continue to do that throughout my life."

Janelle has pondered the political impact of Colin Kaepernick and said, "I just think, as of right now, many people don't like him, but you have to think that people didn't like Dr. Martin Luther King or Malcolm X in their time because they knew that they were helping people and they knew that they were starting a revolution, and that's why he gets backlash. It's because he's getting people to talk, so you're going to have people who love him and people who hate him, but I believe in twenty years, he'll be seen as one of the greatest. He's given people hope. I think that what he did, sacrificing for the greater cause, I just really admire that. If it wasn't for him, I really don't think there'd be a conversation."

One of the inspirations for Janelle and her teammates taking a knee was having a teacher, Jesse Hagopian, who started an initiative called Black Lives Matter at School, where they talked about the political tradition in sports and how athletes were able to bring a message of social justice through sports. "I think that's really what inspired my team, was those people. Especially the girls who took his class, as well."

Janelle looked back at her actions and said, "I think what we did was great. I think what we did also showed a lot of the true colors of people in America, and how much work we need to do. That's the biggest thing I took from that: sometimes when you are sticking up for what you believe in, it upsets people. I really think it showed the divide in America. And when they crack down on people taking a knee or raising their fist, it shows that they don't want people to have hope. Especially being young, you need that hope to keep on going. I just really hope that they don't take away that one freedom people have, to express themselves about what's going on in America. I think that's my number one thing that I took away from it. Any way that you try to express yourself, people that don't like it will try to take that away from you, but you have to persevere and just continue and fight for what you believe in. I'm actually glad I experienced that at a young age, so now that I'm off in the real world, I know and have a better understanding of what people are like and what I'm going to get myself into. I'm thankful and I'm glad that we did that, and I'm glad that we had someone like Colin Kaepernick to give us the courage and give us an example to do that."

The city of Minneapolis usually conjures images of Prince, snow, and an attitude referred to as "Minnesota nice." Almost four years before Derek Chauvin killed George Floyd in this city, Michael Harris took a knee with several of his football teammates at Minneapolis North High School. "Growing up in Minneapolis, you see a lot of stuff. A lot of kids try to use sports to make it out. A lot of people know there may be some gun violence, and that's what people see on the outside, but there's also good about the north side too. It's bittersweet. You grow up bittersweet in North Minneapolis, and you take a lot of pride in it."

For Michael, like so many young people in Minneapolis, the years before the murder of George Floyd had seen high-profile cases of police violence that shaped their childhoods. "Police brutality didn't really hit home for me until 2015, when Jamar Clark got killed by the Minneapolis Police Department," he said. "And then when Philando Castile got killed here too the next year, that's when it really hit that this is real, you know what I'm saying? You really start walking outside and saying to yourself, 'Am I going to come home?' You really start to wonder that."

Michael was a third-generation student at Minneapolis North, a school he loves. He was pushed to take a knee because he was fed up with police brutality, and when he did his own research into the history of the national anthem, he decided that protesting it was his only option.

"People were telling us, 'It might cost you scholarships. It might cost you this or that.' We didn't care. We wanted to make a stand." Six players took a knee for Minneapolis North. A photo of three of them, including Michael, went viral on social media. When that happened, "I was prideful. It was a moment where I thought, 'Yeah, I'm going to stand up for what's right,' you know what I'm saying? I call it our 'Kaepernick Moment.'"

The principal of the school was nervous for the students, but, as Michael remembered, "that didn't concern us. We were going to take a knee. We were going to fight for what's right: racial equality in this country. There was no stopping us."

There were sources of support at the school, which made a

great deal of difference, particularly the Office of Black Male Student Achievement. "That's a group to help with the achievement gap, help with academics and take us on different kinds of college tours. That was my big support system, right there. That's family. I really felt like they were family. There were also students and teachers who would stop us in the halls and say, 'That's what's up. You really stood for what's right. I'm proud of you guys,' and slapping us on the back. I wouldn't say everybody supported what we did, but there's always going to be those that are going to disagree. Everyone's not going to agree with you 100 percent. If ain't nobody's disagreeing with you, you ain't doing it right! But it really felt like it was one of those moments. It was my moment to take a stand and to help my people out."

Michael learned some valuable lessons in this process. "Everybody is not going to always be on your side. But as long as you believe in these rights, you've got to stand for those rights or you will lose them. You will also find out who your true people are. I felt a real togetherness from that. I didn't feel alone when I was taking that knee. I felt like I could always count on those that were with me."

Michael and his teammates felt like they were a link in the chain that Kaepernick had started. "Kap is a legend in the Black community because he took a stand. He really opened up the stage for people to come out and say their piece. He's one of those pioneer-type people."

Taking a stand on police violence is more important than the winning and losing of games. But the year that the Minneapolis North players decided to take a knee, they also won the city championship. "We get to look at our rings and know that the season really meant a lot. We really wanted to bring something to the north side and we did—we brought a championship."

Marjaan Sirdar was an academic adviser for the Minneapolis North High School team in 2016. Originally from Chicago, he is one of the great-grandchildren of Nation of Islam co-founder the Honorable Elijah Muhammad. His family left Chicago when he was a baby, in 1979, to get away from the violence in their neighborhood and start over in Minnesota. His mother was raised in the NOI, but he was brought up in a secular household.

He said with pride, "My family were pioneers in the movement, telling Black people to refuse to fight in the white man's army. Muhammad Ali was a pupil of Elijah Muhammad. My grandfather's younger brother Herbert was Muhammad Ali's manager, so my family was very close to Muhammad Ali. He once married one of my mother's cousins. There's a lot of family photos of Muhammad Ali that I've seen growing up. So Muhammad Ali was a hero to me, as well as Malcolm X."

Mr. Sirdar grew up in the eighties and nineties in the suburbs of Minneapolis, amid an atmosphere of racism and violence. For a young Black child, it wasn't "Minnesota nice."

"It started before kindergarten. I remember when we first moved to the neighborhood, my brother and I went outside to play, two white kids stared at us and said, 'What are you looking at, n——er?' And we ran home and told Mom, 'They called us n——er, what does that mean?' My kindergarten teacher knew my mother was from the Nation of Islam, and she told me, on day one, that I didn't have to stand up for the Pledge of Allegiance. I didn't really quite understand it, but I was like, 'Okay, then I'm not.' So I sat down the whole year, as my peers stood and held their hands over their hearts and pledged the flag. That was kindergarten. Despite the racism I had white friends. I was, for the most part, an active, happy kid. But then I remember the very first day of third grade, a white classmate, white boy, walked by my desk and knocked my book off my desk and called me a n——er. He said, 'Pick it up, n——er.' When we got to the playground, he showed up with two friends. I beat all three of their asses and they became friends with me after that. They respected me. We became buddies afterwards. But that's the shit we dealt with, nonstop, growing up."

Mr. Sirdar has strong feelings about Minneapolis. "I know a lot of people outside see it as like this liberal oasis. It's all bullshit. It's racist as fuck and it's rooted in social and structural inequality. It's a city that will give charity in a heartbeat but doesn't want to share power with Black folks. The north side is a historically Black community, and the poverty and the violence from police is just as historical. Jamar Clark is not really an anomaly. It just happened at a time when national attention was lifting stories like his up. Terrance Franklin was another brother who was murdered by the Minneapolis Police in 2013. This was right when Black Lives Matter was starting to really take shape, the year after Trayvon [Martin] was murdered. That didn't get national attention, but he was a friend of youths that I worked with."

A turning point for Mr. Sirdar and his own desire to stand against police violence was in 1988, when his aunt, a police officer in Chicago, was killed by her husband, who was also on the force. "My aunt Salma, she pleaded for the Chicago Police Department to protect her. They never did. The most they would do is make her husband leave after he beat her, even after she got a restraining order. Anyway, he showed up and killed her. We know that's not uncommon for women and men, no matter the race, no matter the profession, but we know it's more common with police. I was nine years old when that happened. That was the real beginning of my analysis of the police. Prior to that, we had police that would come play football with us, hand out football cards from kindergarten, first grade, second grade, so by the time I was reaching fourth grade, when all this happened, I noticed that white community members treated us differently as we got older. The police started to treat us differently too. We were no longer cute kids; we were seen as a threat."

Mr. Sirdar was put onto his current path when he turned thirty, after his brother died of cancer. He had read the autobiography of Angela Davis years earlier and it influenced him to become a teacher and explore "the revolutionary role that teachers play in our society."

He secured his first teaching job in 2016 at Minneapolis North right before the players on the football team started talking protest. He landed a position working with the program that provided Michael Harris with so much support: the Office of Black Male Student Achievement. "That July," he recalled, "Philando Castile got murdered by the police—eight months after Jamar Clark. So that was fresh on our minds as we're starting class. From my first day in the classroom, my perspective as a social studies and history teacher was to teach through the lens of Black resistance, on and off the plantation. On day one we talked about racism. I opened up with a quote by Stokely Carmichael, talking about how he said, 'If a white man wants to lynch me, that's his problem. If a white man has the power to lynch me, that's my problem. Racism is not a question of attitude, it's a question of power.'"

This began a discussion about Colin Kaepernick, in a class where more than half of the twenty students were athletes. Mr. Sirdar then posed the question: "What if college and high school students participated in this? What sort of movement would come out of it and what sort of demands could we ask?"

It only took a few days until the athletes were done with talking about it and were instead trying to figure out if they could bring this struggle to the football fields of Minneapolis North.

As Mr. Sirdar told the story, "The game was Friday. I was in the stands and so was the principal. A lot of other staff and family members were in the stands as well. The principal did not appreciate my activism, nor did the football coach. So as the administration got wind of what the students were planning, they tried to talk them out of it. They sat them down, I think it was the day before, and they're like, 'Are you sure you want to do this?' They certainly did. I'm there in the stands and I see everybody get ready to stand. I'm sitting, of course, and the principal gave me a mean look. I'm also filming and I see some of the team taking a knee. Originally going into it, they thought everybody was going to do it together, but slowly throughout the week, division happened. The coach and the staff were able to divide the students. Some were scared, so they didn't do it. Some of them just didn't want to do it. There were a few that were like, 'Fuck that, we're not interested.' But many of them wanted to participate, especially after learning about the racist lyrics in the Star Spangled Banner, and they did.

"I was in full support of them, and this led to my demise. I became an easy target for the principal and the coach. Literally,

I'd walk through the hallway and I'd talk to the principal and she'd snub me or roll her eyes. It was real hostile. The coach, who had a lot to say about my role to my students, wouldn't talk to me face-to-face. What I ended up doing—I recorded a short video of the students taking a knee and I took a screenshot of it. I had to send it to my sister to upload it to social media, instead of doing it directly, out of fear of retaliation. My sister posted it, and then I shared it with my network, and I sent it to [journalist and activist] Shaun King, and he ended up sharing it, so they made national news and I was interviewed in the *Star Tribune*, the local newspaper."

Mr. Sirdar's efforts to shine light on the protests and bring in the media brought another world of trouble onto his head. He was moved from North High School at the end of that first semester to a middle school on the south side.

"For me, that was a strong message, and not only from the administration. I also felt tension from my supervisors. One of my own colleagues, who I thought was in support, instead threw me under the bus. I'm a community organizer, a grass-roots activist, I'm an organizer turned teacher, not vice versa. For me, teaching was really an extension of organizing. I'm very intentionally going to organize young people and try to build movements. But that's why they liked me. That's why me going into that classroom and teaching about Kaepernick was no co-incidence. And from day one, I tried to make the connections with my students, 'Who did this before Kaepernick? Who influenced Kaepernick?' Of course, Muhammad Ali came up and I told them my great-uncle used to be his manager. My point was that Muhammad Ali was a hero of mine. Not just because he was the greatest boxer, but because of his activism, because of him fulfilling that legacy of Black folks, specifically in my family, for refusing to fight in the white man's war. Being the embodiment of Black masculinity at a time where a Black boy like me needed that, to fight off white bullies. And I saw that legacy come alive on our team at Minneapolis North. They went on to win the state championship that year, bringing the school its first title in decades. They took a knee in U.S. Bank Stadium before any of the Vikings themselves would have the courage to do so. My students were my heroes."

After George Floyd was killed by the Minneapolis police and parts of the city went up in flames, I returned to touch base with Mr. Sirdar. He said, "Many of us have been predicting this for years. If anybody has been paying attention, the city, this community, had all the indicators. There's a brother named Jason Sole, a criminal justice educator and professor; he said five years ago that Minneapolis is a bullet away from Ferguson. I said that our leaders lack the political will to provide security for Black and Brown people. I said they lack the political will to prevent the city from going to hell. I literally wrote that in an op-ed five years ago. I live four blocks from where Floyd was killed. This is my community. We've been organizing to prevent this. We've been trying to combat gentrification. We've been fighting for a $15-an-hour minimum wage for five years now. And $15 is not nearly enough anymore. We've been fighting for a Working Families Agenda, a comprehensive package to help out working people. Anybody that goes to work should make enough to pay rent and feed their family and take care of their people. We've been saying that and our leaders have said, 'Fuck you.' So hell yeah, we all saw this coming. No surprise. We thought it was going to happen when Jamar Clark got murdered, and then we thought it was going to happen when Philando got murdered. The reason it didn't happen is because we've got some amazing grassroots leaders in the community. I don't mean political leaders. We've got some terrible politicians. Every press conference they give, they lie for the terrorist organization that they call a police department. How much more evidence do we need to say this is a terrorist organization? Donald Trump declares the people who are fighting these terrorists are terrorists. Come on, this can't get any more Orwellian. We saw it coming. The politicians called it a bluff, but they called the people's bluff too many times. Equity would've been cheaper than burning down this goddamn city."

Marjan Sirdar's thoughts then turned to the players of Minneapolis North. "These same people who ridiculed these kids for taking a knee are the same people that say, 'Oh, you could've protested peacefully.' The same motherfuckers who denied equity. The same motherfuckers who forced the governor's hand to reopen the state and send my people back to work, to die for $10 an hour, so they can clip these motherfuckers' nails. These are my youths that are in the streets, on the front lines. These are my youths that are in the 'essential jobs.' These are my former students. They took a knee because their parents have been on the front lines of the wage war their whole lives and they saw it. Their community has been invaded by these terrorist organizations their whole life. Those kids tried to protest peacefully, four years ago. Kap, he tried to take a knee. Now what do they say? 'Why don't you do it peacefully? Why you gotta be looting?' We did it peacefully, motherfuckers. You threw the man out of the NFL and called him and the players that supported him sons of bitches. These young people who took a knee, I'm sure a lot of them are out there protesting too. One hundred percent. And maybe a few of them burning some shit down. The powers that be literally stole land. They extracted labor. They stole people's liberty. They ended people's lives and then they denied them justice. Then the politicians are like, 'Why are you burning shit down?' Then they're blaming us. Order, they're saying, order over justice."

Then Marjan Sirdar said, "The shit that's happening in the streets isn't organized; it's improvised. It's rage. Me and other leaders are trying to organize it—but can we even turn it off if we wanted to?"

The haters say that cheerleading isn't a sport. To the contrary, not only is cheer a sport, it's the athletic face of a school—and when that force takes a political stand, it has an impact that ripples through the entire community. That's true at the collegiate level, as we will see, and it is certainly true in high school. Alexis Reed was captain of the Isidore Newman High School cheerleading squad in New Orleans. "I didn't realize how much New Orleans had an impact on me," she said, "until I went away to college, in Austin, Texas. I realized that my hometown's culture is very different. I love New Orleans and everything about it. The food, the music, the people. It definitely has influenced me. The thing about New Orleans, although we're a great city, the state of Louisiana is not great when it comes to matters of racial justice and incarceration."

When Hurricane Katrina broke the levees and New Orleans was hammered with floods, Alexis was four years old. Her grandmother's house and neighborhood were destroyed and her family's business, a hair salon, was badly damaged. They had to live in Little Rock while repairs and rescue were under way. "Of course, it was very devastating," she said. "It impacted the communities around us, people and family friends, people dying that we knew, neighbors being displaced and just everyone being moved around, having people evacuate from New Orleans to Houston, Atlanta, or just other cities. It was a remarkable time."

These experiences shaped Alexis as she entered Isidore Newman, a private school with a predominantly white, economically affluent student body. (Isidore Newman counts Peyton and Eli Manning among its alums.) "This very privileged white space made me start noticing very small things in sixth and seventh grade," she said, "where now I'm the only Black kid in history class, talking about slavery, and people were saying the N-word and they're looking at me like I'm going to say something, and I had no idea what to do. I started picking up on small, subtle things throughout middle school. When high school rolled around, that's when I really became interested in social justice issues because it was when a lot of high-profile police brutality started happening, around 2015, 2016. That's when it became apparent to me that this was a lot bigger than my personal experiences. It was something that I always felt I knew, but it became very, very apparent, seeing it play out on the news and then going back to school and seeing how people blew it off or how people straight up weren't believing it or blaming the victim, saying things like, 'Well, that person shouldn't have been doing X, Y, or Z.' And seeing how different groups of people, especially those of privilege, handled situations that hit very close to home."

As she was wrestling with all these issues, Alexis went to

Colin Kaepernick's Know Your Rights Camp in New Orleans, in February 2018. It was a full day of historical, nutritional, legal, and financial education, all aimed at helping youth navigate their world. It was an experience that changed her. "I had been contemplating these issues my junior year during cheer season, and my friends and I were thinking about it," she said. "To see Kaepernick talk about his experience and see the other football players that he had there talk about their experience and how they literally sacrificed and put their careers on the line for something that they believed in, and just the issues that they were standing up for, moved me. I thought that if they can put literally their whole career and life on the line for something that they stand by, that they stand true in, I could do that too. That would be a small gesture for me, because I'm just on the cheer team. This is their career. They're in the NFL! If they can do that, then I can do something in my community and spread awareness where I'm at."

Joined by her best friend, Alexis raised her fist as the anthem played before a football game.

"I wanted to raise a fist because if I took a knee, I knew a lot of people would say, 'Oh, she's just trying to follow a trend.' Or, 'She's just doing what Kaepernick is doing, what these other athletes are doing.' He definitely did inspire me, but I feel like raising a fist is also a sign of power and unity and togetherness, and that's something that I wanted to represent. I didn't want it to just be an issue of police brutality, even though that is a huge issue. I wanted it to be about all inequality and racial issues. And I feel like the power fist, that's something that brings a whole bunch of people together, and I wanted that to be our thing."

Alexis was supported by her teammates on the cheer team. "They had respect for me and I had a conversation with them after everything happened. I didn't intend for it to be a big deal. I was just doing what I felt I believed in, what I wanted to demonstrate. I didn't plan on anything blowing up or becoming a big deal, but of course it did! People were offended and all that good stuff. The cheer team itself was very supportive of me. It was probably the administration, the school, and those in power at the school that had the biggest issue."

While there was more than enough behind-the-back sniping at Alexis, there was also the satisfaction of knowing she reached others. "People would come up to me and they were very happy with what I was doing. They'd say, 'Thank you so much for being brave and speaking up against these issues that we've been dealing with for so long.' Because everyone knew the culture of Newman, and everyone knew that underlying it all, there's a lot of issues having to do with race and inequality. So now these issues are being brought up and people are thankful because it was like no one wanted to address it and we actually have someone doing something about it."

While the praise from peers was rewarding, the administration called her and her fist-raising cheer teammates into the office, and they were grilled. This is a constant pattern, with few exceptions. People in power at these schools, regardless of their own personal opinions, become fearful about what "the community"—or donors—will think of such actions.

"They tried to get our point of view first. They didn't reprimand us right away, but they tried to persuade us into doing other things. They suggested a lot of changes. 'Okay, why don't you link arms instead, or hold hands to protest, since it's more subtle?'

"And I said, 'What's the point of protesting to be subtle? You protest to make a statement, to raise the conversation, to start a dialogue. Why are you all trying to change what we're doing to make it less noticeable and hush it down? When that's the whole point of it.' It definitely became tense at times, because we wouldn't conform to the changes they kept trying to make."

When it was clear that Alexis and her teammates wouldn't budge, the administration threw up their hands and suggested that they hold an assembly to explain to the entire school why they were protesting during the anthem. Alexis, far from being fearful, leaped at the opportunity. "So we had an assembly breaking down what we were standing up for and why we were doing it. We included statistics on incarceration rates, racial inequality, and systemic racism. Everything."

In Alexis's presentation, she spoke of Alton Sterling, who had been killed by police in nearby Baton Rouge. She also spoke of the infamous Angola State Prison in Louisiana as a way to get students to understand that they were not dealing with a remote issue, but one in their home state. "We have all these issues going on in our backyard, but it's not affecting their world, so they don't acknowledge it. It's sad, but it's the truth. We said, 'You don't have to agree with us, but before you make your judgments or assumptions, here are the reasons. We aren't just doing this out of emotions. There are legitimate reasons why we are protesting.'" Alexis also talked about the history of activist athletes, particularly 1968 Olympians John Carlos and Tommie Smith. "One of my teachers, every time he would see my friend and me who were demonstrating, he would call us John Carlos and Tommie Smith, like, 'Hey! It's John Carlos and Tommie Smith!'"

The assembly was a rollicking success and inspired the school to hold a Social Justice and Equity Day. Despite that, or perhaps because of that, parents and alumni were calling in with complaints, as did people claiming to be veterans. "They were saying, 'We feel deeply offended. We don't agree with it.' I said, 'The whole point of a protest is, on some level, to make the person, whoever is viewing it, uncomfortable.'

"My thing is, if you can feel uncomfortable in that moment, for a second, then you just get a glimpse of what minorities have to go through, every day, living our lives. It was not my intention to disrespect anyone, but the small amount of uncomfortableness you feel in that moment is nothing compared to my experience as a Black woman in America on a daily basis. Many other Black people feel that same way. Many minority groups feel that way, walking through their life in America. For me, I couldn't feel bad or guilty because, okay, you feel disrespected, but literally, I feel disrespected every day I go to school, I feel disrespected every day as a part of this country, which does not acknowledge my existence."

I asked Alexis what she learned from the experience. She said, "Do not operate out of fear. If you believe in something and if you really, truly hold something to your core values and it's what you stand on, do not let people try to change that or try to make you stray from that. Do not waver in your beliefs, because I think so often, what if I operated out of fear? How would that outcome have been? What if I wouldn't have done something, or what if I changed my protest because that's what the administration wanted me to do? What if all the people who were talking negatively about me—all these alumni and parents—what if I fell under the pressure? The outcomes would have been completely different."

There is no more dangerous place to live in California than Humboldt County. Even with its incredible natural beauty and world-renowned cannabis industry, its rates of poverty, murder, death by firearms, food deprivation, car crashes, and opioid use make it a minefield of social duress. Amid all of this life and death drama, Areli Toscano, a cheerleader at McKinleyville High School, decided to make a stand.

In her overwhelmingly white school, "there's a lot of trouble with racism," she said. "I've been working with staff and the principal and the other students to help bring awareness to issues that are going on, and helping students of color feel more welcomed."

Areli made the decision to take a knee because she saw the conversations that Kaepernick was starting and decided that it was an action that could help her do the same. "I thought, 'Okay, he really has a voice and he's using his voice for a good cause and he's doing it in a peaceful manner. So I started kneeling. I wasn't even on the cheer team yet, but I would just kneel or sit during the anthem all the time. And then eventually, I did join the cheer team and I started kneeling at games, which caught a lot of attention in the community. Being one of the only people who does that and also a person of color, it really drew a lot of attention and a lot of negativity from adults."

Areli was compelled to act by recent cases of police violence in Humboldt County, as well as by the apathy around her. "It's really disappointing, so I felt like I needed to bring more aware-ness, especially in my predominantly white community."

As a result, "I have been called multiple racial slurs, espe-cially the N-word, by other student-athletes and members of the student body," Areli told me.

She made the decision to take a knee without telling her team or coach. "It just kind of happened and every single per-son in the crowd turned their head and looked at me because I was the odd one out: the only one ever kneeling, so all eyes were on me. No one on my team, specifically, called me out, but behind my back, there was a lot of talk."

Areli felt the backlash particularly when she knelt at a foot-ball game. "It was against our rival school on a Friday night. A parent from the other school emailed some staff member, I think it was our principal, letting them know that I should be kicked off the cheer team for not standing. Word got around the school. On Monday, I walked into class so nervous, but al-most all my teachers showed me so much support. They com-forted me and congratulated me for being so brave to do it in our community. That meant so much."

The worst instance was in class when the vice principal's son sat in front of her and told her to "go back to your country." Areli remembered him saying "that if I didn't like how America was being run, that I should leave, and how I have no right to be protesting and how I'm disrespecting the troops. It was very bad. I then told my principal, and then my vice principal was basically crying. She made herself the victim, and so did her son. She was begging me not to speak about it and tell anyone what her son did, because it would be a huge deal for people to know that the vice principal's son acted out in such rage and said such racist things."

The cheer team itself froze Areli out. "We're supposed to hold hands," she said. "Even if I'm kneeling, we're supposed to still be held together. Some girls, or really all the girls, would avoid holding my hand, so I would be there, singled out, and I would just be pushed off to the end of the line. We would line up and I would never be put in the middle because no two people wanted to be right next to me. One girl talked me down to all of our teammates and said how I was being super immature, that I didn't know what was actually happening in America, and that I had no respect for police officers, our troops, or our nation, that I absolutely hated America, which is not true at all. Another one of my team members, her mother had an issue with me. She said I was disrespectful because her husband served in the military, and how I was really throwing out hatred at her family, specifically, which I have no idea how she got that because all I did is kneel. I didn't target anyone. She had a lot to say about me and she told her daughter not to ever talk to me during practice, or during games."

Areli continued to kneel through her senior year, and the emails to the school and the boos from the stands kept coming. While the support from her teachers bolstered her, Areli's parents didn't want her involved in this maelstrom of controversy. "My parents are immigrants," she said, "so they don't know too much about what's actually happening. They really wanted me to stop. I tried to tell them and explain why, but they kind of see it as, 'Why do you want to draw more attention to yourself? Especially in this community, people are going to hate on you.

Why just do it to receive hate?' I would explain to them what is happening. I know there was a case where an innocent man was killed in Sacramento. That hit really close to home because I'm five hours away from there and we have family there. I said to them, 'That could've been one of our family members. That could've been one of our friends. These are innocent people just going about their day and police officers just stopping them and freaking out, pulling their gun out, and killing them for no reason.' That should not be happening, especially if these are trained professionals and we're just normal civilians, not trained to act calmly when a gun is pulled on us. That's what people need to understand."

Niskayuna is a small, majority-white, conservative town of about twenty thousand people in upstate New York. It is a sparsely populated, highly insulated environment, and a joy for retirees. In other words, not a place prone to scenes of revolt.

But in the athletic department at Niskayuna High School, that's exactly what went down.

Ismail Stewart went to Niskayuna High School, where he took a knee while playing football. When he first moved there from Schenectady, Ismail was one of only two African American students in the entire school. "Excuse my profanity," he said, "but growing up in Schenectady, I was used to the word 'n——ga,' because it's more used as a social term. My parents had a problem with it because I came home one day and I asked them, "What does the word 'n——ga' mean?" So my dad, being Black, gave me the very short explanation that it was a profane word: 'Don't use this word.' I had gotten to Niskayuna and this is where I first came across the word 'n——er' with the hard r.

Never heard this term in my entire life. I come home and I'm completely unaware of what this word means now, because it was used completely differently: like, you are this, you are that. It was used as an insult, so I was confused. I came home and asked my parents about that and they gave me the same answer: 'It's profane. Don't use this word.' I didn't really even fully understand what it was, or why it was being used differently and being pronounced differently in Niskayuna."

Ismail was also seeing videos online of white police officers shooting and killing Black men and not receiving any kind of punishment. "It was a clear-cut video of him being shot and the only thing I truly remember is his body running and falling to the ground in this odd position. In the movies that I grew up with, everybody's falling, everybody's dying so beautifully. Fall to the knees, look up to the sky. But not this guy."

Then there was just the reality of being Black in the predominantly white space of Niskayuna. "You almost feel like an anomaly. You feel like you stand out everywhere. You're metaphorically the loudest one in the room just because your contrast is different. I just felt like the spotlight was always on you, so every little thing you do always gets broadcasted. Whether it's good or bad, some people really love the fact that you're different and some people really hate the fact that you're different."

It was exhaustion with this dynamic that finally pushed Ismail to take a knee. "I had gotten tired. I had gotten tired of the demographic in my area. I'm tired of all the kids sporting the Confederate flags in the school. Tired of people in the stands of basketball games screaming the word 'n——er' when they get angry or when someone misses a basketball shot. Stupid things. Some people here hadn't gotten rid of old mentalities." The

Confederate flag particularly got under Ismail's skin. It's been a broader phenomenon in the Trump era to see that flag make the journey north as an all-purpose symbol of white supremacy.

"That flag is technically, at a patriotic level, an enemy symbol. There's no reason why you should even be sporting the Confederate flag in upstate New York. They're reviving this native racism taught to them. As for me taking a knee, I'm getting recognized for football, why can't I get recognized for speaking? Why can't I use this platform to shed light on potentially a bigger issue?"

Ismail wasn't alone in taking a knee. Several Black and white teammates joined him. "We had a whole team meeting," he remembered. "A lot of the team didn't like it. A lot of the team didn't want to do it, but at this point, I felt I had to. It felt like—I don't want to go as far as to say a calling, but I felt that this was a task in this long streamline of life that I had to face: a speed bump that I needed to come across."

At first, the coaches supported Ismail and his teammates. "But then as the backlash started, as people started to ask them, 'Why aren't you disciplining your players?' That's when they started having an issue," he said. "Then the coaches started to say that if we kept kneeling, the school would cut the funding for the team, which we all believed at the time, but I looked into it and learned that the school doesn't even have the authority to cut the funding. I realized, at that point, that the coach had either made that up or the school had told him to say that to get us to stop. Certain backlashes, like the social media backlashes, were a lot worse, because they were a lot more direct and threatening. I received DMs from people on teams that we would play . . . some real tough shit! Some real internet talk."

As with many of these stories, it was teachers who stepped up in this difficult climate and demonstrated solidarity with the players. "The teachers actually showed their support," he said. "They really gained my respect. My initial impression of teachers is usually not bad. But you don't really know after you make a controversial statement, because you essentially part the seas and you have people taking sides. If you're not on my side, then you're my enemy. My teachers would visit me when I would be taking other classes, give me a handshake, give me a hug, and say, 'We're really behind you. We respect you for this.' They were better than my classmates. I had friends that I never talked to again because of taking a knee. You lose some, you win some. A lot of these kids had military parents or military personnel in their family and they felt like I was personally attacking them. But there's nothing about the military in the national anthem, first of all. Nothing. My uncle, he's an army vet, ex–Secret Service agent. He's a true patriot in my eyes. He backed me on this. You're essentially putting words in my mouth if you say that I'm protesting the military or am protesting our flag. I'm protesting the anthem in itself because of what it says, not because of what people think I'm saying."

This happened in 2017, and Ismail now has no regrets. "Two years ago, maybe I would've regretted it. I went through a whole life-altering series of events after this that had caused me to regret all events, but I'd say now, after I've lived through that and after I've been through my hardships, I'd say no, I don't regret it. I did this for a reason."

A bolt of solidarity that helped was when cheerleader Naylah Williams also took a knee, was very outspoken, and took on a great deal of the weight. "Naylah did a very good job at helping to draw away some of the heat, because she was also basically the poster child of the cheerleaders that had done the same. On the same field, on the same day. Much respect."

Naylah Williams had to be fearless when she took her knee. Fans waved Confederate flags behind her back as a way to intimidate her, but she kept her resolve. For her troubles, David Duke tweeted out her name. The KKK grand wizard tweeted a picture of Naylah kneeling with the sarcastic caption "Diversity is our greatest strength."

"It actually got me released from class," she remembered. "I didn't know about it, but my teacher knew about it, so he told me to go down to the principal's office. I asked, 'Oh, what did I do?' He said, 'Go to the principal's office. I'll meet you there.' Then the principal told me, 'David Duke is tweeting out your picture.'"

That tweet went viral, which certainly sent a cold chill up her spine, but as Naylah remembered, "For every bad comment, there were ten good ones." I caught up to Naylah after the police killing of George Floyd. She said, "My first reaction was, I cannot believe this happened again. You hear about something like that, but hearing about it and then watching the video are two different things. So you're like, okay, this is a basic police brutality case. I really cried about this for days. I don't know why this one hurt so much. I think it was because if you look at the police officer's face, he is completely calm, which is different than most police brutality occasions. Then the police officer isn't cool and collected. The police officer is erratic, doesn't know what to do, and then ends up shooting them and there's so many emotions behind it. But Derek Chauvin was completely calm. There was no, 'What am I doing? I need to stop. I'm going to kill this person.' It was, 'You know what, I'm going to kill him, there's nothing you can do about it, and I know that the law is going to protect me.' And it was written all over his face, which is so deeply disturbing. I don't think I've ever seen a police officer so calm, and everybody's screaming, and he just doesn't move, doesn't do anything, while George is calling out for his mom, who's been dead for two years. That doesn't faze you? I don't know when racism got to the point where it was socially acceptable to kill a man and have nobody step in. People shouldn't be comfortable being that racist. People shouldn't be comfortable being racist at all. The comfort of him doing the action, to murder somebody, it was disgusting."

Naylah went to her town's Black Lives Matter rally, and that Niskayuna, given its demographics and politics, even had a rally speaks to the breadth of the movement. Upon arriving at the town square, Naylah remembered that she "was tearing up" because "the same people that said, 'I don't understand why you're kneeling for the national anthem. I don't get it. I don't know what you're talking about' were there, listening to other Black people in the community express why they're doing it, why this needs to change, what needs to change, what we expect from them. It was a very humbling moment for me because I thought about what I did years ago and realized that I'm not alone anymore. People heard what I said. I've had people message me and say, 'I am so sorry. I didn't understand why you did it in high school and I wish I did it with you.' That statement right there is just kind of like, wow, I didn't even think that you still thought about it. But the fact that this happened and you're now realizing, 'This is exactly what Naylah was talking about.' It's sad that it had to get to this level, but at least people are starting to speak up and use their voice."

Naylah defiantly believes that the masses of people who took a knee laid the groundwork for this moment. "I think that it shined a light on a problem, far more than what I thought it was going to. Even the NFL released a statement basically apologizing to Colin Kaepernick. It's jaw-dropping, I think. More so because I was tweeted at by the KKK, and people were talking about me in class. But they were also trying to understand police brutality because they had never seen it happen. They don't know what it's like to fear for their lives when they get pulled over. So for one of the Black people in a predominantly white area to say something about police violence, they used to respond with, 'Are you sure that really happens?' Now people are saying, 'Oh my gosh, this actually happens,' because they've seen it. Now I'm even seeing police officers kneel. Like in Schenectady, police officers knelt with the protesters. To me, that was one of the most powerful moments. I was thinking, 'You're kneeling with us because you see us, you hear us, and now you're starting to realize that you have the power to do something about it.' I've been having so many different conversations with people who say, 'I've never thought of it like that.'"

For Naylah, the number of people in her life who touched base with her in 2020 was in itself life changing. People were going through their own personal reckoning and reached out. "There are folks I went to elementary school with, they're saying, 'Wait, you were going through racism in elementary school?' I'm like, 'Yeah, you don't have to be twenty to be racist. You can be racist at six years old. It's how you're taught. But once you're taught something, you can also unlearn it, and learn to love instead of hate.'"

Osman Rasul also played at Niskayuna High School. He took a knee because "I was expressing, in a peaceful manner, my frustrations. Yes, I got called a bunch of names: classmates coming up to me saying, 'Oh, you're a Kaepernick piece of shit,' and things like that. I took a knee because I'm not going to be that silent majority that will always be like, 'I stand with you, but I actually don't stand with you.' What I mean by that statement is that I wanted to send out the message that I'm totally not just against police brutality, but I'm also against the way the African American community has been treated in our country. I got called a bunch of names. I was called a n——er-lover. I was really surprised to hear that type of language, especially these days."

Osman's only regret is that "I should have done it every game." Osman thinks a great deal about the fact that if people had listened then, maybe there would not have needed to be that explosion of rage after the police murder of George Floyd or maybe even that George Floyd himself would be alive. "What we're seeing now is a huge change. If we look back at 2014, I was fourteen years old at the time and I still remember the issues we were having with Mike Brown in Ferguson, Missouri. They let that officer go off the bat, but obviously it was very tough, because Missouri became the Deep South. What I mean by Deep South is, like, you know in the past there was segregation, slavery, and African Americans were just being tortured and killed on a daily basis. That history is slowly reviving itself."

Osman sees this being actively encouraged by Donald Trump. "When he heard about the football players taking a knee, he responded by saying, 'We've got to get those sons of bitches off the field.' It's very surprising to hear the head of the United States, who's supposed to the be leader of the free world, sound instead like the leader of the authoritarian world."

Lansing Catholic High School is an affluent private institution with very few Black students. When Michael Lynn III, a star quarterback in the city, was asked to come to the school and play, it appeared to be a dream come true. Michael was the first Black quarterback in the history of Lansing Catholic.

The excitement wore off quickly for Michael: "They knew I was coming to play quarterback, but they had kids lined up who wanted that position. It was definitely, like, 'Who is this guy? Who does he think he is?' I'm coming in, this young, sixteen-year-old Black kid, and they thought I wanted to run things. I was like, 'No, I'm just here to play football and have a good team.' It was definitely difficult walking into that environment with all the expectations of who I should be."

Michael received an education in the reality of racism at a very early age. "I was seven or eight years old, playing outside near a friend's house, and he wanted to go inside to play video games, and when we did, his dad, immediately after we stepped through the threshold of the door, said, 'I told you not to bring them n——ers in here.' Obviously, I didn't know all of what that meant, but I knew I wasn't welcome, so I took my little sister and we went home. I told my parents what happened, and that's when they sat us down and talked to us about everything."

There are deep roots to the racism projected onto Black quarterbacks. The working idea for decades—and it persists to this day—is that you need to be a leader, a "field general," to be a quarterback. Such a position of stardom and authority can only be held by white athletes. Black players who have tried to break that particular glass ceiling have long encountered obstacles well beyond the quality of their play. In such an environment, one would understand if Michael had made the decision to keep his head down. Instead he took a knee.

He said, "I'd seen Kap do it, obviously. I was also aware how much I meant to the city of Lansing. I knew, at that time, there was nothing I wanted to use my platform for more than to speak out."

At first his coaches were very supportive. The donors at the private Catholic school, however, disapproved, and pressure was put on the program to cease the action. In addition it became a hot-button issue in the community, garnering a great deal of local publicity and anger. But players started to come up to Michael and say, "I want to kneel with you." That turned into two, then three, then four teammates.

One reason for the support of teammates could have been the response in the stands. "The student section loved it. They kneeled with us. They came up to us after the game and said, 'Yo, I respect you so much for actually doing it, and not just talking about it.'"

That love sustained Michael and the players. But there was still a backlash.

"The backlash came in a lot of different forms that I didn't know it could take," he said. "Obviously, there was the verbal: people yelling stuff from the stands, telling us to stand up. But also, certain people decided that they couldn't be around me anymore. I thought they were my friends, but obviously they weren't. It hurt, but it was a blessing to have any fakeness in my life exposed like that because those are not the type of people I want in my life anyways. Then one time, a man tried to lunge and attack me when I was walking back to the locker room and the police officers had to grab him up and all that. There were other incidents in school also. I am half-Mexican, so I'd get teammates who were against me putting 'Build the wall!' over and over again in team group chats. Those were my teammates, so what do you think the other students were saying? What do you think our opponents were saying?"

Some memories are not so easy to forget or disregard. "I remember like it was yesterday," he said. "We were playing against our rival school. We hate them and they hate us. They took it a level too far, involving me. They were calling me the N-word with the hard r. They were calling me a monkey. When I'd be running the ball down the sideline, I could hear them making monkey noises. We'd be in the red zone, right by the student section, and I could hear it. If I can hear it, I know my line can hear it. I know my wideouts can hear it. I know everyone can hear it, but nobody wants to say nothing. Then I tell my coach, and he said, 'There's nothing I can do.' I'm like, 'What do you mean there's nothing you can do?! Go talk to their coach. Go talk to their AD. Do something. Please have my back for once.'"

It wasn't until afterward that Michael came to grips with the fact that he was shouldering all of this as the school's first Black quarterback, giving his protest an extra level of risk.

Michael recalled speaking, along with several of his teammates, to Kaepernick over Skype after they took their knee and him telling them to keep their heads up. Michael said, "I think he's a lot braver than a lot of people give him credit for. I'm sure some colleges didn't want to recruit me after I did this, but he literally lost millions of dollars over something he believed in his heart. He's one of the bravest people that I've learned about or that I've had the pleasure of speaking to."

I asked Michael if the protests that we have seen around the country in 2020 and the sight of entire teams of pro athletes taking a knee gives him a sense of vindication. He said, "Yeah, when I did it, I was almost alone. Many people around me were for it, but they were silent. I always say, you being a silent ally, you might as well be in opposition. You being silent does nothing. I do feel vindicated, like, yeah, I was right, I told y'all. It's not even just kneeling. It's standing up for yourself. We showed them, whatever cause it is, stand up for yourself. I think us being fifteen, sixteen, seventeen years old, it showed people that they can do it too, whatever age, but especially the young people."

Solomon Mosley attended Carver High School in Atlanta, Georgia. He took a knee at one of the games, as officials yelled at him to get back on his feet. Solomon ignored their snarling shouts because he had a sense of history that he felt a responsibility to carry forward. "My dad used to show me videos about slavery and how Jim Crow laws came into effect." Solomon also remembered being in a mall with his parents as a child and witnessing an arrest. "We saw him get slammed to the ground. They put him in handcuffs, but they were doing extra stuff. That's the first time I witnessed police brutality in person."

Solomon was pushed to take a knee because "I agreed with Kaepernick. At that time, the game hadn't started yet. I was just in the zone and before I knew it, I was on my knee. I was just kneeling and I was just like, 'Hey, I'm going to stay kneeling. I don't want to stand up no more.' When I went to get up, officials were all up on me saying, 'You can't be kneeling.' But I wasn't the only one kneeling. There were a couple more teammates who also had taken a knee and the referees got kind of offended and even wanted to stop the game for a minute there."

Solomon feels a sense that now perhaps people will understand why he acted, because of the explosion of demonstrations that followed the murder of George Floyd. "I feel like the police take advantage. They take their authority to a whole other level, to where they shouldn't take it. When they know they messed up, they don't care. They feel like they've got the right to do what they feel like doing. 'Okay, if I do this, I'm going to get away with it, because there's no consequences behind it when I kill another Black man.' It's so crazy that people didn't start protesting until now, but another Black man, Ahmaud Arbery, was killed not too long ago for jogging while Black here in Georgia. I was like, 'Why didn't y'all start protesting then?' They waited until Minnesota felt it. Then y'all added the looting and stuff, and that's not cool. That's not what we're out there for. I felt like some people took advantage, you know what I mean? But the bigger issue is that there needs to be some type of change so the police can stop killing Black males for no reason. To be real, I have a lot of white friends. I'm cool with a lot of people. That's just me. But I feel like we, being Black men, are singled out from everybody. You've got Black men killing each other.

You've got police killing us. It's just a lot going on and you never know when your time is coming. . . . Sorry to get all serious."

Solomon went to the protests himself because "I wanted to see how it was in person. Just seeing it on TV doesn't really give you any type of real-life experience. They can show you anything on TV. That doesn't mean it's real. For example, they said a lot of people were breaking stuff. They showed a lot of people doing that, but what they didn't show was how they had a lot of bricks stacked up by businesses. I've seen it myself, bricks stacked up in piles. They're really setting people up. You know if people are mad, they're going to look for bricks to bust down windows. I actually saw piles of bricks downtown. I don't understand it. My guess would be that the companies, whoever owned those companies, put them there because they got insurance, meaning they'll get money back. So it's not just 'looters' taking advantage of the situation. It's the businesses as well."

Sterling Smith took a knee in the conservative state of Nebraska as both a football and basketball player at Lincoln Southeast High School. At Lincoln Southeast, "sports were a very important part of our high school program, for sure. And it's a big championship football school as well."

Sterling's first glimpse that the world operated by a different set of rules for Brown and Black people was after the killing of Trayvon Martin. "I had more of an understanding seeing someone so young, that looked like me, in a situation like that." For Sterling, Trayvon's murder animated and then heightened the threat level he felt when dealing with racism's daily indignities.

"I remember one time I was a little kid at the store with my mom at Walgreens, and I was just walking down the aisle looking for candy. Then the manager came up to me with an empty medicine bottle and said, 'Did you take this?' I said, 'No,' and shook my head. He started ripping the pockets out of my pants, going through my pockets. I told my mom and we came back to the store, of course, and she made him apologize to me."

Sterling's motivation for taking a knee was seeing Kaepernick do it during the 2016 preseason. "I thought to myself, 'This is something I have to do in solidarity to him.' Then I was seeing on ESPN that they were talking about the Black Lives Matter movement—these things that you would never in a million years see them really talk about on ESPN. So that really grabbed my attention. You could see it made people a bit uncomfortable, but the discussion had started and that's what prompted me to do it."

Before taking a knee, the first person Sterling told was his dad. "I was telling him and he said, 'Okay, I'm going to support you 100 percent, but are you ready to deal with what comes with it?'"

Sterling felt he could handle whatever was to come. Then he told his coach, who made it clear to Sterling that he needed to tell the entire team. "Honestly, I figured I might be nervous, but when the time came, I really wasn't. I just told them, 'I'm going to do this regardless. I know you may have your beliefs and whatnot, but this is something I have to do, and I just ask that you respect my decision.'"

The reaction of the team was some support, some silence, but an overall response of respect. When Sterling took a knee, another player even did it with him. But after the game, "that's where things got a little bit out of hand," he remembered. "I took the knee and got interviewed about it after the game. My dad also got interviewed. And then, I remember, the very next day, there was an article in the paper. My DMs on social media were just full of mostly people making racist comments or death threats, with only some people supporting me. There were a lot of people that gave me their two cents. I wouldn't necessarily argue with anybody. I would just try to educate them on why. If they didn't understand it, that's the best I could do. I can't force someone to understand something they don't want to understand. I felt like a lot of people couldn't relate because it's not a problem that affects them directly. They didn't really want to understand or try to understand. I also felt like their families influenced what they believed and what they thought. A lot of people tied it to 'Oh, the military, this is disrespectful to the military.' Well, most of the family on my dad's side has served in the military and then a lot of my old teammates actually went into the National Guard. I remember talking to my ex-teammates about it and they said, 'We support you and we understand why you're doing it.' I wouldn't change doing it ever. Not in a million years. No."

Sterling took something precious from the experience. "All it really takes is one person and there can be a ripple effect that's *ginormous*. It can lead to a lot of good things. No matter how negative the effects of it might be, the good will outweigh it any day."

Seeing the protest explosion after the police murder of George Floyd made Sterling feel even better about what he did.

"And it's super ironic, to me, right now, because that was so controversial for people to take a knee. They said, 'That's disrespectful, don't do that.' And now people are taking out their anger and their pain and the trauma, and the response has been, 'You guys should be peacefully protesting.' Well, we tried that, and that wasn't good enough either, so what else do you want from us?"

2

College

Few workers are at once more powerless and more powerful than the college athlete. College sports are a multibillion-dollar operation, with tentacles across the financial, social, and cultural life of a campus. The so-called amateur student-athletes— particularly in the revenue-producing sports of football and men's basketball—are expected to live, eat, and sleep the sports that they play. The head coaches make seven- and even eight-figure salaries to command these operations, and at many schools they are far more powerful and influential than the school's presidents, provosts, or deans. The president of Ohio State was once asked if he would fire the head coach and he responded, "I only hope he doesn't fire me!" In roughly forty of the fifty states, the highest-paid public employee is either the state university's football or basketball coach.

Meanwhile, the players in these revenue-producing sports are treated like indentured servants: no wages for the billions they produce, no collective bargaining rights, no ability to improve their health care. Athletic scholarships, which at most schools are renewed on an annual basis, can quickly be forfeited. You could be class president with a 4.0 GPA and if the coach decides you are gone, then you are yesterday's news.

The student-athletes who bear the brunt of this precarious situation are Black. They make up the overwhelming majority of the athletes who play football and basketball—as much as 70 percent of the athletes who take the field. They are the ones in a position of powerlessness relative to the head coaches who lord over the programs. It is an unjust system that, when the smoke clears and the ragged, jagged melodies of the fight songs fade, is little more than a mechanism for the theft of Black wealth. Consider the wages that these college athletes could be earning and the communities where that money would go. Instead it funds an NCAA that seems to exist only to enforce rules that ensure compliance among the programs and make sure that some of the nation's top athletes do not see compensation for what they produce.

Yet these same athletes also have a tremendous amount of power when they have the vision and gumption to exercise it. So much of a school's financial portfolio now depends on these sports; they are the tentpole of the modern neoliberal campus. And it isn't only the school that depends on them. Most big-time football and basketball powerhouse schools are in small college towns like South Bend, Indiana; Tuscaloosa, Alabama; or Gainesville, Florida—towns that have become dependent upon the success of these teams as well. Everything from hotel occupancy on weekends to kids selling water bottles by the side of the road rests on the foundations of what is supposed to be "amateur" athletics.

Because so many economic levers get pulled only if the athletes play, their power, should they choose to strike, is overwhelming. We saw this in 2015 when the football players at the University of Missouri made the decision to refuse to take the field unless *the university system's president, Tim Wolfe, stepped down. They flexed this power only after Black students and white allies had protested for weeks, following a series of racist incidents on campus. The school learned that it would have to forfeit $1 million a week for every game that was missed. All of a sudden, Wolfe's position as university president was expendable and, along with the chancellor, he was gone.*

More recently, we have seen Black college athletes organize themselves and speak out, inspired by both the movements after the police murder of George Floyd and their concerns about being forced to play amid the pandemic. Their efforts have come after a summer when high-profile coaches like Mike Gundy of Oklahoma State and Clemson's Dabo Swinney found themselves in hot water with their players and programs for, at best, being tin-eared about the demands and aspirations of the Black Lives Matter movement and, at worst, preening from the wrong side of the police line. All of a sudden, some coaches were in the hot seat, the power dynamics dramatically altered at long last. Other coaches, like Nick Saban at Alabama, actually took part in a racial justice protest through his college town that was led by the entire Crimson Tide football team. The same kind of march took place at Mississippi. Just consider that for a moment: Alabama and Mississippi football players marching for Black lives. It is truly a bold new world. The plantation system of college football is facing a reckoning like none we have ever seen before. It's the pandemic. It's the racism. It's the absence of economic justice. And it's a volatile combination that could change the system forever.

The groundwork for the current moment was laid by the people in this chapter: athletes in a whole range of sports who bucked this deeply oppressive system where there is very little chance to be heard. It is without question difficult terrain: no union, no parents to have your back, and the end of your scholarship dangling over your head. But these athletes should be understood as a political weather vane, signaling which way the wind is blowing to an obstinate power structure that is only now beginning to listen.

The University of Pennsylvania is the Ivy League school of choice for the Trump family and many other elite students. The Philadelphia-based college is also where Alexus Bazen was a cheerleader, after growing up in Thomasville, Georgia, a small southern town in the southwest of the state.

"Thomasville is just a tiny place in the Bible Belt. Growing up as a young Black woman in south Georgia, it was what it was. The town has a three-hundred-year-old oak tree that they used to hang Black people from. It's a crime to tear it down and it's right in the center of the town. If you go downtown, there's no way you're not going to see it. That should give you an idea."

Other than the occasional Mexican migrant workers, Thomasville was Black people and white people, sharply divided. "I was always privy to racism," she remembered. "My parents made sure to teach me about the things I would experience, some of the things I would see, and why people act a certain way: why I couldn't go over to certain friends' houses or why people would say certain things. The approach toward racism in Thomasville was that 'racism doesn't exist here.' But it's very much woven in the thread of the culture of the town and embedded in its history. Even to this day, I haven't been home in years. I'm still friends with people on Facebook, and I see that some still have certain negative mentalities or certain negative ideologies, and it's unfortunate. Thomasville is a beautiful place. It has a very hometown feel and everything like that. But would I go back and raise a family there? Probably not."

When Alexus was a child, the brother of one of the members of Alexus's church was traveling near Tallahassee, Florida, just thirty minutes from Thomasville. He was driving with a suspended license and was pulled over. Somehow that turned into him being killed, shot "eighteen to twenty times" by the police.

"For me, I was very young, so I couldn't necessarily grasp the gravity of that situation, but as I got older and started to see," she said, "I understood what systemic racism was. I saw it in school. I saw it the interactions I had with people. It began to really click in my head. I think what solidified all those experiences was Trayvon Martin. When Trayvon Martin was killed it divided my town. Trayvon's case was not police brutality, but it was racialized violence. All my Black friends were saying, 'It was wrong. [Trayvon's killer] had no business doing that. Trayvon Martin lived there.' My white friends said, 'Well, he deserved it. He shouldn't have been sneaking around the neighborhood.' They were blatantly ignoring what I was saying, which was that this was where he lived and he was unarmed.' He was walking back with freaking Skittles and an iced tea, a snack that I myself enjoy. I also liked to take walks up to the corner store with my friends, so I identified heavily with him. To hear my white friends ignore all of the evidence to justify this vigilante who was told by 911, 'Don't approach this kid,' it was confusing at first. But I went from confusion to anger to frustration to just, 'Okay, I get it.' I think that was the first time it really clicked with me. My reality as a young Black woman is just worlds away from my white friends. It made me question those relationships and question, 'Okay, where is my place in this? Where do I fit in?'

"I knew this was racism. I knew this was institutionalized violence. I knew this was wrong. Then, at the same time, I was a top-performing kid in my class and all my white teachers were like, 'Oh, you're so different from everybody else.' I think it was a cascade of understanding that racism is so much more than being called 'a n———er,' which I have been called, to my face, in my hometown. It's so much more than that. It's in our schools. It's in the way parents talk to our kids. It's in our ideologies. It's in our justice system. I still, to this day, have moments where I have to really sit and process, like, wow, my white friends saw that incident completely differently than me and my Black friends. Not only that—I don't think they understood how terrifying that was for us, you know what I mean?"

Alexus has two younger brothers, and after Trayvon's killing, she started to fear for their lives. "Even now, I'm getting flustered talking about it," she said. "It was one of those things where it just shook me to my core. Everything I thought I knew about race, everything I thought I knew about race relations and diversity . . . That could've easily been me. That could've easily been one of my brothers. How can my white friends not see that it's not safe to exist as a Black person in this world? Maybe I'm being dramatic, but to this day I still feel every time my brothers tell me they're going out, or my Black friends tell me they're going out, I play the respectability politics game in my head, asking myself 'How do they look? How are they dressed?' I really shouldn't have to. I don't believe in respectability politics, I think it's bullshit, but it's the way we survive. The fact that we can't even thrive and we can't even survive."

The case of Ahmaud Arbery, killed while jogging in rural Georgia, hit too close to home as well. "I moved back to Georgia recently. I go out and I go running. To think that just existing as a Black person—not even getting to the fact that Black women who are murdered and who experience violence don't even get the airtime that Black men get . . . that's a whole other issue. It's just living in fear. That was the biggest wake-up call that I had."

For Alexus, these feelings collided with the ways that she was elevated in white spaces. "I'm going to be real with you. I was always pedestalized as the 'ideal Black person' by the white people that I was around because they would say things like, 'Oh, you're nothing like them. You're smarter than them.' For me, it created an internal conflict. I'm not different from 'them.' I *am* them. When people found out I got into Penn, they used that as an excuse to go even further and say, 'You're nothing like those other people.' It created a complex in me. Because I knew that no matter how smart I am, no matter how many Ivy League degrees I get, no matter how light-skinned I am, you look at me and I'm still Black. I'm still subject to racism. There was nothing special about me that was going to save me or protect me from racial violence and police brutality."

It was the accumulation of all this history, all of this weight on her shoulders, that led Alexus to take a knee at Penn, but her reasons were also more tactical. "I did want to ruffle some feathers and get people talking. A lot of people said, 'Oh, you live this privileged Ivy League life. Why would you have any-thing to complain about?' Which is complete and total bullshit, because nothing about me is privileged. I grew up poor. I grew up in a single-parent household. I went through the mud to get where I am. But I wanted visibility. Now that you've seen me kneeling, you're talking about me kneeling. Let's talk about the reasons why I kneel. Let's talk about Trayvon Martin. Let's talk about Sandra Bland. Let's talk about Korryn Gaines. Let's talk about Philando Castile. Let's talk about all of it."

Alexus also felt a particular responsibility to act because of her experiences as a Penn cheerleader. "I felt an obligation to do it because even on my own team there were instances of microaggressions from teammates and little things that were said and done," she said. "This couldn't continue and I needed people to see, to really see this. If it takes me getting on a knee, getting people riled up to at least start the conversation, then I'll do it."

Alexus also acted because football held a place of great ac-claim and attention on campus and she did not see any of the players ready to act. "As somebody who was involved with social justice work from the moment I stepped onto Penn's campus—and as one of the few Black cheerleaders on the team—I felt it necessary," she said. "None of the football players were going to do it. Black football players would commend me, yet unfor-tunately I think they were so afraid of what would happen to them if they did it. But I'm not a coward. I told my coach, 'If you want to kick me off the team after this, fine by me, because you know what? At least I started the conversation. At least I brought attention to it. I may have ruffled some feathers, but you know what? At least I had the courage to say, "No more, this is wrong."' And it's funny because the sports world profits off of Black bodies so much, but as soon as you step outside of the sports world, we're nothing."

Alexus's coaches were actually very supportive of her. No one was going to be kicked off the team. Her teammates largely were there for her as well. "My coaches really understood why I did this," she said. "There was an incident where a bunch of Penn freshmen were put into a group chat, and they were being bombarded by racist messages, racist imagery. A couple of my 'cheer babies' were affected by that. For a lot of my teammates of color, I got a lot of thank-yous. 'Thank you for doing this.' 'Thank you for taking a knee.' 'Thank you for really sticking up for us and bringing visibility to these issues.'"

While the campus culture was also largely supportive, there was a backlash that came from the outside that went about attacking Alexus on social media. "There were people who said, 'You're disrespectful to the flag and to the people who fought and died for this country.' That made me laugh too, because I come from a military family. My mom, my dad, my uncle, my brother, my grandmother, my grandfather. Literally, like, my whole family is military, are veterans, you know what I mean? Veterans fought and died for my right to be able to express myself the way I want to. And honestly, how unpatriotic would I be to see a problem with the way my country is treating my people and not call attention to it?"

But people claiming that Alexus was antimilitary was the least of her problems. "I did receive death threats, unfortunately. I also had people come to my dorm and leave things at my door," she recalled. "It must have been students because the dorms are pretty secure, and you have to have a student ID to get in. But it didn't deter me. It didn't scare me. I may have pushed the backlash out of my mind, because for me, there's nothing you can do or say to me that hasn't already been done or said. If I have to die over taking a knee or if I have to experience violence—whether it be verbal, physical, whatever—because I took a knee, then that's okay, because people have died, literally, just for being Black. To me, the backlash was just a small sacrifice. A small inconvenience. My mom was scared for me. My family was scared for me. My friends were scared for me. I did have people distance themselves from me because they didn't want to be associated with my actions and what I was doing. But I want to be on the right side of history. I want, when my judgment day comes, to be able to say that I fought for equality in this country. I fought for a nation where my children and my children's children can live without fear of being persecuted for their skin color, or their gender, or their sexuality, or their identity. I have a family rooted in social justice and activism. My grandmother was a Black Panther. It's in my blood. It's my calling, and I felt that it was, especially with the platform that I had, my responsibility to do something. If it was something as simple as taking a knee, and if I were to get crap for taking a knee, then, oh, well, that's just what I have to do."

Alexus felt a particular responsibility as a Black athlete, because among the other teams, any kind of activism just was not present. "I think Black athletes at Penn took the [stance of] 'I'm not going to get involved because I don't want to lose my place' or 'I don't want to get kicked off my team' or 'I don't want to cause issues.' They just kind of put their hands up and didn't want to deal. For me, I thought, 'Okay, Colin Kaepernick could easily lose everything. He was willing to risk his entire NFL career to bring these injustices to light. What do I have to lose as a college cheerleader?' If he was willing to put all of that at risk, then there's no reason why I shouldn't. There's no reason why I can't. The combination of having access to that platform and already being involved in social justice, how can I take this to the next level? I just took advantage of the 'privileges' that I had."

One "privilege" that Alexus also had was that her parents made sure to educate her about John Carlos, Tommie Smith, and Muhammad Ali—athlete-activists themselves—so she knew the hidden history of struggle expressed through the sports world.

"I think I already had the passion and what Colin Kaepernick gave me was the action," she said. "Here's my equivalent to raising my fist. Here's my equivalent to not wanting to be a part of the draft. It's so simple, getting down on one knee, but it speaks volumes. I've done what I can do as a student. I've done what I can do as a member of these social justice organizations. Now here's what I can do as an athlete, to bring it over to the sports world. My only regret is that I didn't do it sooner."

Alexus believes that if you are an athlete and you have a platform to call out police brutality, use it. "Use it because it matters," she said. "At one point there were little kids who were out there on the field. At one point one kid kneeled next to me. There are kids who are watching. There are young folks who are going to have to grow up in this world. I don't want them to be afraid to call out injustice. I don't want them to be afraid because of whatever backlash they might experience. If you have a platform, if you have a voice, and if your voice can be magnified for a good cause, for a good purpose, for making this world a better place, then do it. There's nothing more detrimental than silence. There's nothing more detrimental than saying, 'I'm too afraid. I don't know what's going to happen, so I'm not going to do it.' Imagine if Malcolm X had said that. Imagine if Medgar Evers had said that. Imagine if freaking Angela Davis had said that! Imagine if all of the activists who shed blood, who gave their lives, said, 'You know what, I'm too afraid of what's going to happen, so I'm not going to do it.' I couldn't even picture what this world would be like. I know not everybody has the same personality. I'm a no-nonsense, bold, straight-up type of person. I was willing to deal with whatever negativity and whatever backlash and whatever sacrifice. I was willing to do that. I just think that we have to be bold enough, we have to be brave enough, and we have to have enough forethought to not be silent. Because silence and complacency are the biggest sort of detriment to equality, and to a world we can live in—where we can coexist and live in peace."

The best reward was when Alexus had cheerleaders who joined the team after she started kneeling who said, "You know, I came to Penn because I heard about you. You're the kneeling cheerleader and that was a big part of my decision."

It can be a struggle for antiracist activist-athletes in a city or even a liberal college town. Now imagine doing it in Storm Lake, Iowa, an area known as "Steve King country" after the former white supremacist congressman who was voted out of office in 2020. Alyssa Parker, hailing from the comparatively big city of Des Moines, took a knee at tiny Buena Vista University, in Storm Lake.

"I was born and raised here in Des Moines," she said. "It's

always been good. I have both of my parents in my life. They both actually got remarried when I was young, so I was raised by four parents. It was really a small, tiny school district and I was the only Black person in my graduating class. So that experience, I think, shaped me into the person I am today. I learned a lot about my own identity as a Black woman."

At the start of high school, a story hit the news that rocked Alyssa: the killing of Trayvon Martin. "That's really the first moment, for me, I can vividly remember feeling this intense passion or desire to just do something. That's where my journey began."

After high school, Alyssa matriculated at Buena Vista, where she met an upperclassman, and they started the school's first Black Student Union. It was at a BSU meeting during her sophomore year where the discussion turned to Colin Kaepernick. The ascension of Kaepernick as a social justice figure coincided with conversations about Jordan Edwards. He was a young Black man who had been shot and killed by police while riding in a car after leaving a party. Alyssa's frustration after hearing about Edwards's death boiled over. "I thought, 'We have to do something! We can't just keep having BSU meeting after BSU meeting. It's just the seven of us listening to each other. We have to do more.'"

The bulk of this small BSU was comprised of cheerleaders and football players, so they decided to use the platform that they had and take a knee during homecoming.

"It was me and three or four other cheerleaders on my cheerleading squad," she remembered. "Then there also were four Black football players, so we all took a knee at that game. It was, like, silent, dead silent. I guess I didn't know what was going to happen. I thought we had done something good and we were all happy with what we did, but the aftermath of it was downhill from that night. Afterward we went out to celebrate with our fellow classmates. But we weren't very welcomed to the homecoming festivities anymore."

If that Saturday's homecoming ended with a series of uncomfortable interactions, by Monday it was bedlam. A social media beehive and local news coverage about their actions led to donors and alumni threatening to pull money from Buena Vista. The new school president called the kneelers into his office. "He really was genuinely open to hearing why we did what we did and what he could do to help," Alyssa recalled. "That's what it came off as, originally. We chatted, we gave him some ideas. But he also asked the question: 'Is there another, alternative protest you guys could do?' He knew his donors and his community weren't very happy. As the spokesperson for the protest at the time, because I was the BSU president and it was my initial idea, he had also asked me personally if I could get the group together to find a different kind of protest. I kind of just politely told him, 'At this moment in time, I don't know if there's another protest. And us conforming because people were upset kind of takes away the point of the protest.' He wasn't very happy about that and I get why he wasn't happy. There were people that were outraged, not just in the school, but in the community and in Des Moines, that were reaching out to Buena Vista, saying that this was not okay. I think the pressure of the negative reactions was weighing down so hard on the president that he just kind of chickened out."

A few days later, Buena Vista's administration sent out an email forbidding protest, in any form, while in a Buena Vista uniform. That didn't deter Alyssa, however. "I thought that if we stopped now, they're winning. It would take away from what we're doing. We had to keep protesting. But as we started to talk—we talked to our cheer coach and the boys talked to their football coaches—the boys said they were done. 'Oh, Alyssa, we're out. We can't not play football. We only *came here* to play football. I'm sorry, but we're done.' I said, 'Okay,' and I went to my fellow cheerleaders. I had a couple girls that were on the same page as me, who also thought that we had to keep going, but a few of the other girls only went to Buena Vista to cheer and the punishment of protesting, in any form, was being kicked off the team. I tried to think of my options. I loved cheer, but I was never going to be a professional cheerleader. It wasn't a life-or-death situation, and I felt like what I was protesting was exactly that. So I told them all, including the president, 'I'm still planning on protesting this Saturday.'"

After Alyssa made this clear, the school president then put out another notice that kneelers would not only be kicked off the team but "sanctioned and punished in other ways," via a "special committee." Alyssa was pushed to the point where she resigned from the team but still showed up to every game to kneel in the stands. Even that didn't calm the haters. "People were coming up to me threateningly in the stands. They needed police officers and extra security near me. They were getting calls to the point where the school officials were genuinely worried about my safety. It was crazy. The news was all over this story, which was putting pressure on the university president, because it was starting to go national once I resigned. BET picked up the story and Colin Kaepernick retweeted about me resigning from my team."

The intensity of the reaction against Alyssa included being shunned by several of her professors, leading her to worry about her grades. She also had classmates who wouldn't speak to her. Yet this crackdown on the protest ended up attracting national attention to what could have been a local story. The ACLU got involved, eventually giving Alyssa an award for her courage. "I didn't realize this was going to be my fifteen minutes of fame, I never would have guessed that when I started doing it. My story was getting posted everywhere—it was crazy, I was losing track."

Through protesting, Alyssa started to research and learn about the history of demonstrations and struggle in sports. "It made me realize it's bigger than me. Even though I'm in Iowa and in a small town, this protest really did make an impact. I couldn't let my anxiety about being safe stop me. I had to keep pushing. I'm not losing a gold medal, like other people who protest lost things. I was losing cheer. But to me, it felt like I was losing nothing compared to what I was protesting for. I think that's when I really started to learn." Alyssa even communicated with other athletes thinking of taking the same step, and they would be a source for one another of advice and comfort. "I just thought it was so cool that there were other people, really from all over the world, doing the same thing as me."

Yet none of the positive attention changed the fact that Alyssa was in the land of Rep. Steve King. The day before finals of that same semester, she woke up to a racial slur written on her door in permanent marker. "At that point, it just felt like maybe this wasn't the place for me," she said. "I'm a sophomore in college and I can't even go to sleep, wake up, and take my final without feeling like I was in danger. I thought, 'Who's going to be here to make sure nothing happens to me if my own university is throwing me to the wind?' That's the point where I felt like I had to transfer. Although the protest was very meaningful to me, I felt like I could still protest and make an impact at another university and also not fear for my safety. I was so distracted. I had to remember that I was also there to get a college degree."

Alyssa was also starting to feel that the protest message was getting lost: the story had become about her and riling up this little Iowa town. In the end, Alyssa felt like she had to switch schools and transferred to Grand View University, in her hometown of Des Moines.

"I tell people all the time, I really wish I came here all four years. It's not even much bigger—it's still private; it's still kind of small—but the people here are just different. I think because we're in Des Moines, it's just more diverse. It is more experienced and more willing to just have those conversations. We're going to argue, we're going to fight, I'm going to protest, and we're going to go back and forth. I started the BSU there, and in our first year we won club of the year. They gave us money for the group. The school is just more helpful. I think they actually care about pushing the message that I was fighting my university to talk about. I think they're more willing to help me push that forward and I think that's critical. That was important to me in a university, to know that they would at least have my back."

Many of the stories in this book happened with little or no media coverage. What went down with the cheerleaders at Kennesaw State University in Cobb County, Georgia, is an exception to that. Kennedy Town was one of the cheerleaders who took a knee in Cobb County. She is another person whose formative years were shaped by the murder of Trayvon Martin. "It just hit really close to home, because I have four brothers, and it scared me to think about how they could be walking down the street and then get killed for no reason. And then with the police brutality, just the different stories that you hear in the media, the different videos that you watch, that opened up my eyes. One situation, specifically, that shook me was when there was a Cobb County police officer that was recorded telling this woman to not be afraid at a traffic stop because they only shoot Black people. That's really what started my passion for fighting for awareness in the hope that change would be made."

Being a student-athlete was a fun life at KSU, but all the good times shifted dramatically after Town and four of her teammates took a knee. "It sparked a lot of controversy. When I saw Kaepernick do it, that's when I said to myself, 'Okay, this is a protest about an issue that I care a lot about.' Then I saw that another cheerleader at another school ended up taking a knee, and I thought, 'Wow, she's really brave.' That is when me and the other girls got together, and we realized that we shared the same passion. We had to think long and hard about it, but we decided to do it, and I absolutely think we made the right decision."

Kennedy was certainly scared, especially because she was going to school in Cobb County. "It is a very racist place," she remembered. "I didn't know what type of retaliation we were going to get. I knew it was coming; I just didn't know to what extent."

The cheerleaders took extra care to make sure that their actions were kept as a surprise to everybody. "Only us five knew, and a couple of other Black girls from the team," she said. "We told them about it, but not everybody made the decision to take a knee with us. But with my team, they were all very supportive, even if they didn't have the same views we did. They said they respected our opinion and they respected what we did."

The school was also largely supportive, with faculty members reaching out to offer their solidarity and students coming up with their own different kinds of solidarity protests and asking how they could help. It was social media where the backlash truly began to fester. "Take Twitter," Kennedy said. "We had an article about us out on Twitter, and people were responding to it with all sorts of nasty things, like we should only be on our knees for one purpose. Or if you don't like it, leave America. Just people putting us down, calling us all sorts of names. After the online harassment, when we all took the knee, it became a regular occurrence that the crowd would yell that we should only be on our knees for one thing. So we didn't only get the racism, we got the sexism too."

But even with the community support and the vile nature of the backlash, the dean of the school, in conjunction with the Cobb County sheriff, wanted them off the field. After that first game, they had to wait in the tunnel during the national anthem and then run out on the field afterward.

"When we first heard about that change after practice, I knew immediately it was to keep us from taking a knee. I felt like they were trying to silence us, but it didn't work, because even in the tunnel, we were taking a knee. There were some photographers still taking pictures of us in the tunnel. It showed them that they can't stop us, they can't silence us, they can't change our minds from what we believe in."

Students were not having this kind of crackdown on the cheerleaders, and there were protests on campus against the dean's decision. "He had a ceremony on the green, and so over one hundred students came and took a knee during his festivities, to show that they stood with us. It was so moving. I just felt happy that I had a support system behind me, because up to then it was a lot for the five of us to take. Knowing that we had our campus behind us, it really felt good."

One reason that this protest of five cheerleaders at a small college was garnering so much national publicity was because Kennedy and her teammates were doing it in Confederate country. "Confederate flags are everywhere," Kennedy explained. "So seeing five Black girls taking a stand against police brutality, it probably really triggered them. It was such a powerful story that the media had to report on it."

Kennedy had to get ahold of her fear in order to forge ahead. "I didn't know what type of retaliation we were going to get. I didn't know if we would need to face down very real, actionable death threats. I didn't know anything. I just had to go by faith. But I wasn't going to let strangers affect my views or make me scared."

Kennedy learned a great deal from the experience. "I learned that your voice can be heard. You have the right to a freedom of speech. If you are passionate about something that's going on in your country, you have a right to stand up for it. No matter what type of backlash you get, what type of support you get, as long as you're happy with what you did, that's all that matters."

Because of the social media attention, students from as far away as London reached out to Kennedy. I was like, 'We made it to London?!' It was just so crazy." An organization of families of vicitims of police brutality even gave the cheerleaders an award. Still, it wasn't easy. "It was very overwhelming, with all the different press interviews. It became a lot to handle. I was definitely concerned about doing it and getting my name in the media, because I know there may be people who don't have the same views as me, and that could mess up my chances of getting a job. Other than that, I don't have any regrets. I'm proud of what I did. I'm proud of the outcome and I would not change anything."

Howard University is perhaps the most prominent historically Black college in the United States. It sits in the heart of DC: not the DC where politicians and lobbyists ooze from one five-star steak house to the next, but the DC known as Chocolate City, the home of go-go music, Marvin Gaye, and Duke Ellington. Howard's place at the center of this community meant that when the cheerleaders took a knee, the ripples flowed through the parts of DC where the bigwigs fear to tread. One of those cheerleaders was Sydney Stallworth. Sydney is from Odessa, Florida, a largely white, tightly knit community. She closely followed the story of the killing of Trayvon Martin and then the denial of justice when his killer walked free. "That made me realize that our legal system is not always fair. It's not always just, and that was a rude awakening."

Sydney turned down the opportunity to stay close to home and attend Florida State University, instead taking a leap of faith by traveling to Washington, DC, to attend Howard. "The cheer team was my first family on campus," she told me. "Those girls, my teammates from my freshman year to the girls that we brought in when I was leading as a senior, they are amazing. We're family. Nothing less. It was an awesome experience. The games are a social event. Everyone looks forward to them—not necessarily to see the team sometimes, but just see each other. The camaraderie: the band, the cheer, the dance. It just has that HBCU game-day energy. I think that's what really drew me. At first I was swamped with school and cheer. That's all I did: school and cheer."

The team decided that they wanted to be the cheer squad that would take a knee; they started kneeling at every game and just kept on going. The kneeling began the year before Sydney became co-captain, along with Alex Jones. The captains before, who took the initiative to kneel for the first time, were Sydney Harris and Paige Stiger, when Alex and Sydney were sophomores.

Before Howard games, they play the national anthem and then what is known as the Black national anthem, "Lift Every Voice and Sing." The cheerleaders would go on one knee for the national anthem, and then, for the Black national anthem, they would stay on one knee and raise their fists.

The support they received not only at Howard but in the broader DC community was overwhelming. "One time I was getting coffee with a friend and saw my face printed up on the billboard behind the barista," Sydney recalled. "That was crazy, to see me and my teammates up there so that everyone could see what we were doing."

Every time a new class of cheerleaders came into the

program, Sydney and others would talk to them about why they decided to kneel and why it was important for them to do it as a team. Then they would ask the first years if they would like to be a part of that. "If they didn't want to, they could have the space to stand," she said. "But I can't remember a time where anyone stood, mostly because we hashed it out in those conversations beforehand, or everyone explained how they felt and nobody felt any differently. I think that going to an HBCU, a lot of people think that maybe everybody is the same, that all of your classmates think the same, but we're so different. We come from places all over the country and have all kinds of ideas, but it's good to know that we can all recognize when injustice is being done."

Today, Sydney has no regrets for kneeling, but she does deeply regret that they could not have done more and that her actions wouldn't be relevant today.

"Look at everything that's going on in the world," she said. "Minneapolis is burning. George Floyd, that video of him being suffocated in the street is breaking people's hearts. It breaks my heart. It's like, how many more people have to die? How many more videos have to be shared? This is not individual incident by individual incident. This is systematic injustice.

"I think being a member of the Black community, it's just that. You're part of a community. Going to Howard, you're completely supported. I'm getting emotional talking about this because I wouldn't have gotten that anywhere else. It wasn't an accident that I ended up at Howard; it was a blessing. They teach you that your opinion is valid and they give you the space to vocalize it. I'm just thankful for the space to be able to speak my truth and say how I feel and know that I'll be judged only on the validity of my arguments, not by what I look like."

It is said that the state of Nebraska doesn't need any professional sports teams because they have Cornhusker football. It's treated like the only game in town, and it is a state obsession.

Michael Rose-Ivey played football at the University of Nebraska for five years. It was during his fifth season that he took the knee, a decision that was informed by his entire life experience. "I'm originally from Kansas City, Missouri, where I live currently," he said. "I've got six brothers and sisters and I'm the oldest. I grew up around both my mom and dad, but they had me when they were fifteen. They were never married but were together through high school. Living with my mom, she dealt with some abusive relationships, things like that. There were some bad spots, living-wise. Football allowed for me an escape from those types of situations."

Michael knew that police brutality and racism were an issue before he ever knew the name Colin Kaepernick. "One of my first experiences I can remember, we were living in the inner city and a cop just pulled up on my friend and me and asked if we stole a bike. We were nine or ten years old. I also had an older cousin with me, who was thirteen, and they handcuffed and roughed him up a little bit because he was being a smart-ass. That was probably the first moment it clicked. Their power is different than mine. That badge has a different presence, a different aura that allows them to do things others cannot."

Another time was when a police officer followed his parents to their home because he assumed their car was too expensive for them to be driving it. The officer came to their front door and demanded to see proof of ownership. "This is a small type of thing, but within it is 'the big scare': the fear that a small incident could turn deadly. It starts to change you."

At Nebraska, a school where Black Americans make up roughly 5 percent of the student body, the racism weighed on him, even as a high-profile football player.

Michael's reputation as a political person who was outspoken about police violence had teammates asking him if he was going to kneel before he had even thought about it. "We had Mike Riley as our head coach at the time," Michael said. "He's a West Coast guy, so he's a lot more laid-back, a little bit more 'liberal,' if you want to say that. I had spoken to him about it the night before the game. I told him more than I asked him. I said, 'Hey, Coach Riley, I've been thinking about this. I've got teammates asking me about it, and I'm going to kneel tomorrow, during the anthem.' He said, 'I would love for you to do that. Go ahead. I think this issue is something that needs to be discussed and I think Nebraska would be a great place to get that talk started.' He was behind me, 100 percent. Three of us originally did it for the one game, and then I did it for the whole season."

Before taking that knee, the issue of fear was very real, no matter his political confidence in what he was doing. "I guess I was scared, but I was more nervous than scared," he said. "I remember the announcer saying, 'Please rise for the national anthem and presenting of the colors.' Then hearing fans go, 'Get up! Get up! Get your ass up! Respect the flag!' and more yelling from the stands. The first time we did it, I had two guys with me, but then the rest of the season, I was by myself. I could only do it for road games because at Nebraska, we don't play the national anthem while we're on the field. So the first game, I had two guys with me, and then by the last of them, I was the only one, but I had security protection standing next to me."

Then came the backlash. The Board of Regents wanted them off scholarship, effectively kicked out of the school. Social media was a hotbed of threats. Michael had extra security for road games. The governor of Nebraska spoke out against the kneelers, further inflaming the moment. Michael even had to meet with the FBI because of what was seen as an actionable death threat on Twitter. A man detailed how he was going to come to the stadium and slit Michael's throat. "It got crazy," he told me, "but for the most part, I think it definitely helped spark some type of talk, which is the main goal of protests. Let's get conversations started and let's find ways to turn the conversation into solutions."

During this time, social media wasn't only threats of violence. It also forged a connection between Michael and some high school football players who saw him explain to the media about why he was kneeling and were inspired. "I spoke to a couple of kids from Eastern Michigan [University]. They had kneeled; I spoke to some high school students in Lincoln. There were a lot of high school students reaching out to me, saying, 'I saw your speech, I'm kneeling too.' I thought that was awesome! It just sucked that they didn't have the support that I had, especially at the high school level. To be able to support those kids, because you saw a lot of stories of kids getting kicked off teams, or had their playing time reduced, all this other crazy stuff."

As for the threats to take away his scholarship, Michael said, "I wasn't surprised. I was disappointed. They said that since I was using the knowledge that I attained at the university to justify my actions, then I was misrepresenting the school, which is the biggest load of bullshit you could throw out there. We met with the chancellor and the dean of students and they calmed our nerves by telling us, 'There's no way in hell we'll let you guys get kicked off the team or out of school.'"

But the most hurtful backlash was what taking a knee did to Michael's NFL chances. He came into his senior season as the fifteenth-ranked linebacker in the country, had a stellar senior year despite all the turmoil that engulfed him, and then went undrafted. Michael was in the Bears rookie camp and then was cut. "I'm not saying it hurt my opportunities in the NFL or anything like that, but it definitely didn't help me secure a career. I think God works in mysterious ways and he put that on my heart for a reason. I look at it like, maybe I'd be playing, but now I'm pouring what I know into these young men and young people as a coach and trainer. That's what I'm doing now, and it's a blessing."

I returned to Michael several months after our conversation to ask about the police murder of George Floyd. "It was so disheartening," he said. "You can't justify that someone's a threat when you literally have your knee in their back. I think there's so much symbolism there, with Kap's kneel, and the way this police officer went about taking a man's life from him: hearing him scream for his mother, who wasn't there. Me being a spiritual person, I felt like she was right there with him, calling him home."

Michael is now taking his own action. "I met with a really large group of Black men, here in Kansas City. We have decided we are going to start some type of program where we're educating our young Black boys and girls. For one, about our history, and two, the true history of this country. Just being a presence of power for people in the community. I appreciate everyone that did go out to a rally or protest, because they were able to push the needle. It's very needed in any form, however you can, to create disruption of the system. It's definitely much needed."

I asked if he felt that his actions laid the groundwork for this explosion of struggle in response to Floyd's murder. He said, "The groundwork has been laid by the labor of our ancestors. The groundwork was set by the people that came before us and were assassinated, or had been forced to remove themselves from this country, due to the idea that they're a threat to what the foundation of America is. I think that's important. Like I said, I'm just a small part of the flame."

I asked if he felt any sense of vindication for his actions. He said, "Not really. It's an eerie feeling that all these companies and people are coming out and speaking on behalf of the movement. As for the demands that are out there, what does defund the police actually look like? What does de-escalation training actually look like? Those are the things I'm really looking forward to seeing. That's why I'm trying to figure out how best I can be a part of that change, here in Kansas City. I have my hand and mind on that, in order to help the next generation."

He then spoke of the cost of this moment. "There was a time, a week and a half ago, where I was just completely drained. Just from this stuff and getting back to work on a full-time schedule, it was just tough. For you, for myself, everybody who may get a chance to hear this, just take care of your mental health. Make sure that we're maintaining ourselves spiritually, physically, and emotionally, so we can't be swayed or altered by the moment."

Arkansas is a very conservative state that also suffers high rates of poverty, income inequality, and segregation. It is also a state that hadn't seen its share of protests in the years leading up to 2016. Into that void stepped Jordan Danberry and several of her teammates at the University of Arkansas. Danberry is from Conway, Arkansas. From an early age, she received the message that for her, as a Black woman, what people referred to as "acting hostile" toward police was not an option. "I just knew this from my own experience with my family having to deal with police brutality and the justice system overall. I just knew that police treat people a different type of way and there's nothing you can really do about it. There's nothing that you can change, there's nothing that you can really say to change their mind about the person you are to them."

Danberry was inspired—or provoked—to take a knee because she was exhausted with the drumbeat of stories of Black people being killed because of racist violence. "I thought about how I'd seen Kaepernick using his platform and thought, 'That's something I could do as well. That's a platform that I can use where it will get someone's attention that what's going on in the world is not okay. It's not right.'"

Before taking a knee, Jordan talked to her teammates. "I asked them if anybody had an opinion about kneeling and wanted to join me in taking part in a silent protest during the national anthem about racial inequality," she recalled. "The conversation that sparked was not really what I expected. I thought some of my teammates would be on board because of prior discussions. We talked about this topic a lot, and I just knew that they would be taking a stand with me, but then when it came time to actually do something, many of them decided not to. We had some people that were just dead set against it. It really did cause division. But most of my teammates, being who they were, stood by me having the freedom to have my own opinion and right to take a knee."

Now that Jordan had decided to do it, the fear factor came into play. "I was a little terrified. Just being from Arkansas, knowing that this is my home state and being the person that I was to a lot of people back home, it was very difficult. When you bring up race, it's always a tricky topic. I guess I felt like I was a little scared that people wouldn't look at me the same, or they wouldn't like me, or they wouldn't do whatever it was that they were doing for me at the time. But I got over that and made clear that I had to do it because this is what I believe. And then I had people that wanted to do it with me, so that kind of eased the fear a lot."

Fortunately, back in Conway, Jordan had a great deal of support. "I actually had a lot of love behind me back home, especially my family and my friends," she said. "People that were close to me were there for me through it all. I had so many people reach out. Even some of the fans at Arkansas and some of the boosters were saying that they were with us. A lot of military veterans as well. It was definitely calming to know that vets did not feel disrespected. They always expressed to me that that's what they were fighting for—for me to have the freedom to express my beliefs."

As for life on campus, "I definitely did not feel like I got support. It came to a point where I stopped going to a couple of my classes. I didn't want to go because of all the stares that I was getting. We were *the* topic on campus. Threats were coming in from online and I just didn't really want to be around anything like that because I was in northwest Arkansas and that made me feel vulnerable. For those who don't know, northwest Arkansas is way different than central Arkansas. Central Arkansas has a lot more African Americans. There's a lot of white people in northwest Arkansas and they had much stronger opinions about what we did."

Jordan feels even clearer about her reasons now than when she took her knee in the first place. "The reason we wanted to do it was to shed light on racial inequality in the justice system today. It's covered up and it's not talked about nearly enough. It doesn't matter if the cop is Black or white. It doesn't matter if the person that's being targeted is Black or white or any other color; it's wrong. Police brutality is wrong. I feel like they abuse their power and aren't really trained properly. It could be better; it could be a lot better. They could be held accountable for a lot of their actions, and they're not. I just feel like that's something that needs to be discussed. Badly."

Maryland-born Gabriel Sherrod took a knee while on the football team at Michigan State University. "I grew up in a predominantly Caucasian community. The high school that I went to was 98 percent white. The neighboring town, which is Rising Sun, Maryland, is actually one of the biggest known KKK hotbeds of the sixties, seventies, and eighties, and it's still acceptable around there to do KKK meetings and marches."

"One time I played a basketball game at Rising Sun High School," Sherrod told me, "and two of our best players were out. I was the young gun on the team, a decent player at the time, but I had my breakout game. I scored thirty points, and on the way to the locker room, I was called a n——er by several people. And that was the first time that I really knew that racism was not only real, but something that could affect me in my daily life. Here I am, fifteen years old, going out on the court to play a game that I love, and because I did a good job, I get called a n——er. That was the first time that I was like, wow, this is real. It was in my face. It was personal. It was something that's indescribable: the first time that you get called that because you can feel the hatred behind it."

Gabriel had a great experience at Michigan State but was strongly affected by what was happening away from the field, particularly the police choking Eric Garner to death in Staten Island, New York, and his final words, "I can't breathe."

"By that point, it was one of those things where a lot of people were getting killed by the police. I felt, in my heart, that it was only right that somebody stood tall with the victims' families and let them know that we stand beside you. We're here. We support you. Your efforts to get justice for your children, for your brother, for your cousin, nephew, don't get unnoticed by the world."

The stage where Gabriel chose to make his feelings known could have hardly been greater. It was Big Ten football, on the Big Ten Network: Michigan State versus Wisconsin, the number eighteen team in the nation versus number twelve. But there were no nerves.

"I had it set in my heart to do it," he said. "One morning I had woken up, when all the incidents were going on, and I just said in my mind, this is what I'm going to do. I actually tried to get some of my other teammates to do it with me. Two of them did. Several who said they would did not. I guess they just froze up. That's okay; that happens. It changed my life, but no, I was never nervous about it. I was prepared and ready to do it."

Michigan State's coach, Mark Dantonio, publicly and privately supported him, but Gabriel felt like the fan base and the boosters absolutely did not. "So here I am, one year left of school, one year at Michigan State to try to get to the NFL, and in my personal opinion, I think I was blackballed—and so I stopped playing after that. I had plenty of practice film where I was destroying our first-team offense. I believe that I was blackballed out of playing."

Gabriel believes he was hurt by the part of Michigan that Michigan State calls home, East Lansing. "It was another predominantly white area with people who—I wouldn't say are racist. I would just say it was filled with people who think that I should've just stuck to playing football," he said. "That was the reaction that I got across the board from fans at that time: that I shouldn't put my nose in societal issues. I'm a one-year guy, coming into the program brand-new, and then I'm out there raising my fist for something that they really don't understand. Especially if they can't relate to it. It was a nice little bit of backlash. I'm not going to lie. I remember getting on Twitter after the game and people saying that my scholarship should be pulled. A number of fans said that I didn't deserve to wear the Michigan State jersey. It didn't bother me. At this time, I'm twenty-two years old. I've been through college. I've been through backlash, I've been through ridicule. It was just amazing to see people loudly express their point of view on a serious issue which they really can't relate to. Of course, the only thing they can say is that I'm misrepresenting the school. It was very eye-opening to see where people's loyalties lie. It was more important to them to win a football game than to stand for something that was happening to people in our society. I mean, if it was four white kids that get killed in that same time frame, I mean, honestly, what do you think would happen? It would be an uproar. Seriously. And as it should be! So why is it okay the other way?"

The experience taught Gabriel some lessons, namely, "just to not be afraid to speak up when everybody says to be quiet. There are too many times in society where we choose to stand quiet, to please others, to keep our jobs, to maintain our lifestyle. But you have to stand for something, because when you stand for something, you'll never fall for anything. In doing what I did, I was able to appreciate who I was as a person much more because I knew that there was something more in me than football. Yes, I had my math degree at the time, so I knew that I was an educated young man, but that extra moxie in me came about after I raised my fist because it challenged the social norms at that time. It put me at the forefront of an uphill battle that African Americans and minorities are still fighting to this day. I'm truly grateful that I could be a part of something like that."

While playing Division I hoops at UC Santa Barbara in 2016, Mi'Chael Wright attempted to organize her team to take a knee—and faced a hellacious backlash for her efforts. But her journey to that point started in first grade. "There was this boy named Adam who had a class birthday party. He said I couldn't have a vanilla cupcake. He literally said, 'You can only have a brown cupcake. Chocolate cupcakes for chocolate people.' I cried. My feelings were hurt. It wasn't like 'he was mean to me because I'm Black.' My feelings were more hurt because my friend wouldn't let me be happy in this space where we were always happy together. We would play LEGOs together, we'd go to class together, we'd play outside together . . . and all of a sudden it's like there's these rules and regulations on cupcakes."

Police violence became known to Mi'Chael growing up in Los Angeles County because of the story of the 1991 police beating of Rodney King. But she felt the need to act as the stories, videos, and social media posts began to mount starting in 2012 with the murder of Trayvon Martin.

"It was Trayvon and a whole host of cases. I started noticing how other people were addressing these situations. I didn't hear outrage. I heard, 'Well, what was he doing to get shot? What was he wearing? Where was he? What did he look like? How big was he?' With the Sandra Bland case, it hit particularly hard. 'Well, she shouldn't have been so aggressive. She shouldn't have done this, she shouldn't have done that.' You don't get to kill people for having an attitude with you, right? You don't get to kill people for walking home from school. You don't get to kill people for playing with toy guns in the park. That's not something that happens. We need to stop normalizing 'These people should have done something different,' when that's not the case."

Then in the summer of 2016, it came to a head. "Alton Sterling was killed in July. It was Philando Castile the next day. Literally twenty-four hours apart. A couple months after that, we had Terence Crutcher, who was shot on the freeway. Again, hands up, walking back, doing everything he was supposed to do, and still managed to be shot and killed."

Then Colin Kaepernick started taking a knee and Mi'Chael and some of her teammates said, "Oh, this is something we could do. Athletes are doing this."

Mi'Chael went to her coach as team captain and said that the team was discussing taking a knee. At first her coach was respectful. "We talked about it. She wasn't for or against it. She appreciated the conversation, was open to listening. It was very neutral. At the time, I was like, 'Okay, she's with it! She didn't say no.' That's what I heard."

The six Black girls on the team were all in. A team meeting was called to get full team unity, but unity was not in the offing. "We literally watched four Black people die at the hands of cops that summer alone. We said, 'This isn't something where we can just stand by and do nothing. We've talked about it, as the six of us; this is something we're really passionate about and we hope you're on board." But most of the rest of the team was not on board. Mi'Chael suggested other compromise options like holding up a Black Lives Matter sign or wearing black sashes on their uniforms, but every idea was shot down. "They basically came out and said—I remember the quote—'I'm not against it, but I just think there's a time and place, and what about the military?' I said, 'We're not even talking about the military! That's not what's happening and you know that.' So it was tense.

"Then, the day before our first game, the coach decided that she's not going to tell people that they can or can't do anything. So if you want to kneel, you can. If you don't want to kneel, you don't have to. We weren't happy about that because we really wanted this to be a united front. But for her to say, 'You know what, do what you want,' okay, we'll take it. It's not perfect, but we'll take it."

Come game time, six Black players knelt along with two white teammates. Everyone else stood. That was expected. But it was the reaction in the stands that shocked Mi'Chael. "This isn't UCLA or USC. We had small crowds. Many of our boosters and fans had been fans for thirty-five years and been supporting us for thirty-five years. But they started booing us. They threw trash on the court. People were flipping us off. People were leaving. This is, ironically, during the national anthem. I'll never get over that. What you're doing is the exact same thing you don't want people to do. If we're being honest, our stadium was pretty empty anyways, so when our twelve top fans instantly left, it was even worse. I couldn't believe it. I've known these people forever. I've been to these people's houses. They come to all our events, they cook us team dinners, all kinds of stuff."

The next day, there was a team meeting. "This is literally where shit hit the fan. We were all in a room and our coaches said, 'Why don't the people who didn't kneel start.' We didn't even realize that this is what the meeting was about. We were blindsided. I'll never forgive or forget two of my non-kneeling teammates who said, 'We think it's inconsiderate that you're kneeling, because you didn't consider how it would affect us. Like people come to us and ask why we aren't kneeling, and why we don't believe Black Lives Matter, and we have to figure how to explain that to them.'"

The team had become completely polarized between those

who knelt and whose who did not. "People were crying. I said, 'You guys don't even understand how we feel. It was always "no" from you. You didn't want to kneel. You didn't want a banner. You didn't want us to hold anything. You didn't want us to have patches on our jersey. You didn't want us to have black stripes on our jerseys. What do you want?' Another girl said, 'It's just not the time or place. We can do all of these things, but they don't have to be during the national anthem.' The meeting ended with a lot of people crying."

The next couple of games, they knelt. "We got booed, people left. Same thing always happened." But there was a change when the team traveled to Seattle University. "Two other players kneeled with us and people in the stands kneeled and some people clapped for us. We didn't get that at home. We literally got more love and respect shown in an away gym than we did in our own gym. It meant a lot to us. I remember that moment. 'We can do this; we're going to be okay. It's not going to be easy, but we can do this.'"

The drama went on. "Boosters threatened to pull money. They threatened to stop coming to games. Then we were told, 'Well, now you're putting our scholarship funds in danger.' It was a lot of stress for any athlete. I stopped getting invited to people's houses. Our athletic department basically said publicly that they didn't support what we were doing."

This was when Mi'Chael's relationship with her coach really started to erode. They were talked into not kneeling from December 1 to 16, but on December 14, when they played UCLA, three girls on their team knelt. "I think for all of us, at that moment, we realized, we might really just be getting played. We can't believe that we let our coach talk us out of something that we were so passionate about doing. We believed you. We fell for it. So we went into Christmas break and when we came back, we were kneeling, period. That's what was going to happen. After Christmas break, our coach asked us, 'Have you all reconsidered your whole kneeling business?' This is really where we kind of hit a tension, and I don't think our relationship ever recovered from this, really. She started yelling at me, a senior captain. She yelled at me like I was a child, saying, 'You don't understand how disrespectful this is and what you're causing the team to go through.' I think we all literally walked away from the huddle. Now it's just blatant disrespect. You have no regard for us as your athletes, right, but as people, as women, as Black women. You don't care. You don't care, and that's what it is."

The kneeling players were now on their own with no support from their coach or their athletic department. So they decided to go all in. "One teammate and I got together and we said, 'Okay, we're going to plan a *social injustice awareness* game in a month. We'll have a written statement, we'll kneel, and we'll get people to come and kneel with us. We worked hard on that statement. When we went to away games, we dedicated thirty minutes of our time to planning this, before bed checks. We were dedicated. We were going to make this happen because it was something we were passionate about, but it was also about our pride. We were hurt too much. You didn't want to listen. You didn't want to give us respect. So now we're going to show you."

Much to the chagrin of Mi'Chael's coach, the "social justice game" was a mammoth success. "I recruited my mom, my sister, my partner, my roommates, my housemates at the time, to pass out our statement outside, when people were coming into the gym. We had other people's parents passing them around as people were sitting. Big numbers of people showed up wearing black. We kneeled during that game. We had one side of the gym filled up with supporters, and they also sat the whole time during the national anthem. For once we didn't feel so alone and isolated. It really, really, really meant a lot to us. I think we lost that game. Our coach, afterward, said, 'We lost because people were focused on other things and not the game.' Again, it was one jab after another, honestly. It was too much."

Their relationship was done, or so Mi'Chael believed. After graduating, Mi'Chael made her way to the University of Minnesota for her PhD. After the murder of George Floyd and the subsequent Minneapolis uprising, her coach reached out. "She was calling to check in on all the Black kids, asked us how we were doing. So sorry that we're going through this and not all cops are bad. . . . She literally asked me, 'So what do you . . . is antifa really there? How about this new boogaloo group? Are you seeing people in the streets? How's the National Guard?'"

Then the coach put out her own statement that ended with saying "Black Lives Matter."

"I found out from another teammate that she was telling people, 'I did more research, and I was able to learn more about what Black Lives Matter really means. I wasn't sure then, but I'm more sure now.' That wasn't going to do it for me. That's not okay. You didn't know what Black Lives Matter meant then—as opposed to what? You thought it meant something else? What could it have meant then that it doesn't mean now? So yeah, to see now these statements, some of them are performative publicity statements. It's not just our coach. These very people who didn't even want to have a Black Lives Matter poster—even to hold a poster—these same people are now posting statements, and not one BLM post, not one 'defund the police' post. Not one 'We stand with these people.' I instead saw black squares. Everybody was doing the black square thing, but not BLM posts. For my own mental health, I had to unfollow a lot of them. It's not okay. I don't need this performative, fake energy. One of the girls said, 'Oh, I'm reaching out on Twitter to ask you what you think I can do to know more and be better.' So I just ignored it. It's not me. That's not my role. That's not my job. I don't do that. It's a lot different than someone genuinely asking, 'What can I do to help people in the streets of Minneapolis? How can I use my privilege?' Those weren't the questions. You can tell when the questions are genuine."

I asked if she felt vindicated by the uprising for George Floyd, and Mi'Chael took a deep breath. "Yes and no. I think part of me believes that it took way too long. We're here and people are sending out statements left and right, you're sending out statements but still don't have any Black people that you hire. Starbucks sent out a statement. Starbucks was literally in the news last year [in 2018] for calling the police on Black people. I think for this situation, in general, especially with my coach and the current teammates, I think it's a little bit of 'I told you so' but also 'I don't believe you.' Not that people speaking out now isn't important, but it's a fad. It's easy, it's expected for people to be tweeting BLM right now. It's expected for people to be saying, 'Arrest the cops for Breonna Taylor.' It's expected for people to be posting about George Floyd. But then people were against us and against us hard. Hard. They weren't supportive. They didn't care. They didn't want to listen to us.

So I'm proud of what we did, and I'm proud of how we did it. I'm proud we never gave up on ourselves and never gave up on each other."

Division II and Division III athletes have a very different experience than their Division I counterparts. They don't receive full athletic scholarships. Instead, they get either nothing or partial athletic grants of varying size. They are also less of a cash cow, but that doesn't mean they are not relevant to the financial, social, and cultural life of a campus. At many of these schools, because of their small size, sports actually can play an outsize role. That also means when an athlete speaks out, it can send coaches and administrators into fits of fear because any controversy might offend a well-heeled booster, which means trouble for everyone down the line, and shit—as they say—definitely rolls downhill.

Jay "Jenysis" Battle was twenty-three years old at the time of our interview. He grew up in Columbus, Ohio, the oldest of four children. He also grew up playing basketball. Jay was raised by his mom and had to learn how to cook and care for his younger siblings. Jay's father served in the Gulf War and came home to battle drug and alcohol addiction. Leading others was a part of growing up, especially as his mother worked double time to make sure everyone in the house had what they needed. "I did have to do some of the cooking," Jay said.

Jay attended Baldwin Wallace University, a school surrounded by some of the most affluent suburbs in all of the greater Cleveland area. "Definitely a PWI [predominantly white institution], but they had a pretty strong students-of-color presence on campus. It was super organized, a ton of unity amongst all the students of color. Honestly, I didn't really have any bad experiences at first."

What propelled Jay toward taking that knee was the police killing of twelve-year-old Tamir Rice, a killing that took place "literally twenty minutes away from my dorm on the south side of Cleveland. It was crazy. I was a freshman in college when that happened. I overheard somebody in the student union cafeteria saying, 'We're going to go protest right outside Prosecutor Tim McGinty's house.' I heard the address and typed it into my phone. I was with my boy Orlando, sitting at a table eating food. I said, 'This is twenty minutes away! Let's get bundled up. Let's just fucking go, bro. Let's just do it.' All year we were saying that we gotta stop just talking about it and start being part of the culture and really stand up for our people—whether it looks good or doesn't, whether our friends accept us or they don't. So at that moment, I just had an epiphany. I said, 'Let's just go!'"

When they went to Prosecutor McGinty's house, Jay and Orlando were confronted with counterprotesters sitting in lawn chairs with German shepherds straining on their leashes.

"I would never compare anything to the civil rights demonstrations that were happening in the sixties, but I could feel the past in the present when those German shepherds were barking at us as we were chanting outside. It literally felt like a movie. We sat down and lay on the sidewalk in remembrance of how long Tamir Rice lay on the sidewalk until the ambulance got there. It was some powerful shit, man. Right then and there, that's when my life changed."

That was November 2014. It was less than two years later when Kaepernick started kneeling and Jay felt the need to do the same. After telling his coach and teammates, Jay was surprised that the vibe was positive. He had their support. Now it was time to do it.

As Jay remembered, "The first game was at Case Western Reserve University. If you know anything about Case Western, it's one of the more elite Division III schools in the country. The Cleveland Museum of Art is literally right next door. The cream of the crop gets into Case Western. So when I went there and I kneeled, it was wild: everyone was staring, phones were out. I had a shitty start to the game and I just knew my coach was probably thinking, 'Dude, you're distracted. We're going to talk about this after the game. I don't know if this is the best fit for you and our team.' But then after a slow start, I balled out."

Jay's team was almost entirely white and had "zero knowledge on the topic, but as the year went on and as the locker room became closer and closer, I led those conversations and the team ended up taking this dialogue outside the locker room, having them on their own. It also made a great difference that my head coach, Tom Heil, and assistant coach Brian Schmidt always had my back. By the time I graduated, I was super proud of where some of my teammates had gotten to, in terms of being allies to people like me and other Black students at Baldwin Wallace."

The students on campus, particularly the Black students, treated Jay "like I was some sort of celebrity. It was great. I would be lying to you if I just said, 'It was cool.' I took every compliment like it was a hundred pounds. It was amazing to get support from those students. Honestly, the best compliment I ever got in my life was my junior year, when I was still kneeling. This kid from the opposing team—at Thomas More

University out of Kentucky—he came up to me and said, 'Yo, the fact is that you have the balls to do that and our own school won't even let us do it. Dude, I look up to you and I wish I could do what you do.' I was like, 'Bro, that's bigger than basketball. That's bigger than school. Bro, that's bigger than life for you to say that to me.' Just comments like that made me keep going."

There was less solidarity on campus among the white students. The overall dynamic "was definitely a ton of support on one end and a ton of scrutiny on the other."

During his senior year Jay started student teaching at Medina High School, one of the biggest high schools in the state of Ohio. "They are super conservative, super loaded with money, and super close-minded," recalled Jay. "The day before school started, I went in and met with my cooperating teacher. He took me to meet the principal. I have two forearm tattoos on me. They stand out, and it's the first thing you see when you meet me. He looked at me and said, 'I don't know where you're at with your tattoos, but I would suggest covering them up if you want to work in this district.' That was the first thing he ever said to me! Obviously the first day of school, I wore a polo and made sure all the students saw my tattoos."

Senior year was also a time of triumph. Baldwin Wallace won the conference championship and ended up making it to the NCAA tournament. With that, there was a ton of news coverage on BW's men's basketball team. A legendary Ohio sportswriter named Terry Pluto wrote an article about Jay in *Cleveland Magazine*. As Jay recalled, "I think the title was 'Baldwin Wallace Guard Jay Battle Kneels Before Games, Leads During and After.' It was probably a two-page write-up on me kneeling for the anthem. Then the comments blew up. I had people threatening me, saying they would 'meet me' at parent-teacher conferences at Medina High School. I had a person say that I'm going to be in the principal's office tomorrow for spreading radical, socialist ideas amongst the students and 'there's no place in a teaching position for a radical leftist to teach kids.' Oh, it was crazy, man, but I loved it. I really did. Obviously, none of those people had ever seen me teach. I had so many kids grow in the right way. Not forcing them to be pro-Kaepernick, but pushing them to be open-minded."

Jay said he taught his students "y'all can believe whatever you want to believe, but I don't want you dissing Kaepernick just because you don't agree with him. Find out why he's doing what he's doing. Ask questions, do your own research, and then formulate your opinion."

If there is one lesson Jay has learned from all of this, it is that "at the end of the day, there's nothing your white friends, or my white mom, can do for me other than support me. I think the biggest test of allyship is what you can bring to the table with getting nothing in return. I think that's where I'm at in my life right now. Trying to help other groups out, with zero intent to get anything back. That's the goal."

Mynk Richardson-Clerk took a knee at North Central College in Naperville, Illinois, as a member of the women's lacrosse team. For Mynk, it was the unjust murder of Trayvon Martin in 2012 that brought police brutality to the forefront of Mynk's mind. Then it was the relentless build up through high school: Michael Brown, Sandra Bland, Tamir Rice, Eric Garner. All of this pushed her to act. It was the summer of 2016, when Mynk was entering college, that Philando Castile and Alton Sterling were both murdered, and that finally changed her irrevocably. "That's really what caught my attention. I was planning on going into college, studying maybe English or journalism, but once I got in, I decided to do political science so I could get a better understanding of the systems that have been oppressing groups of people from all these different periods in history. That really influenced my whole college career."

College was isolating for someone coming into consciousness in Naperville, at a predominantly white institution in a predominantly white area. "The athletic community at North Central is very strong, but it's not very woke at all," Mynk said. "It's very white and almost—culty, to be honest. If you're on a sports team, that's all you can do. The expectation is that your teammates are supposed to be your best friends. You have to eat with them, hang out with them, go to their parties, all this mandatory team bonding. We had to go to sporting events even if we did not want to. That included men's lacrosse games, basketball games, baseball games, and so on. That's where you're supposed to put all your time, but I wasn't like that. I was involved in other areas on campus. I was very involved in activism. I was involved in our Black Student Association. I was part of our diversity club. My team just wasn't a safe place to be able to talk about those issues. I would try to bring things up and they would ignore it or I could see them visibly get uncomfortable, so it wasn't an environment that was conducive to supporting activism, or supporting people of color. It was just not a not a good place to be. It was like that even outside of sports. Even in the dorms. Unless you were at the office of multicultural affairs or at a BSA meeting, it was very tiring, very draining, and very hard to just exist. It's really ironic that they expect you to spend all of your time with the team but do not take the time to understand you as a whole or the social issues that impact you."

When the shootings of Black people such as Jordan Edwards made the news in 2017, Mynk knew that it was time, no matter how uncomfortable she was with the athletic department, to take a knee. Mynk then took a knee for every single game. "My sophomore year came around and there were rumors going around that players on the football team and student leaders on campus were going to take a knee at one of the games," she recalled. "I was also doing marching band then, and when the day came around, I was in my marching band uniform, and I told the band director, 'Hey, I'm going to take a knee and I'm not playing the anthem for this game.' He said, 'Okay, that's fine.' But then, just one by one, everybody bailed. The whole entire team bailed. The student leaders said, 'No, we can't do it.' I remember being so disappointed and so frustrated at the administration as well as the football coaches for discouraging all of them from taking part in the protest.

"It wasn't until later that I learned that the administration and the coaches discouraged the football players from taking a knee and persuaded them to link arms on the field instead. I was angered at the boldness of the administration to persuade a team that had so many players that were willing to protest away from doing this. They were talked into linking arms for the BLM cause, but when it came time to actually do it on the field, an announcement was made that they were linking arms for the Vegas shootings that had occurred around the same time. The original message to protest police brutality was co-opted through the efforts of the administration. This was especially frustrating because these coaches put in so much effort to recruit Black players for their football teams, basketball teams, and track teams but then do not put in the same effort to support the Black players holistically, especially on social issues that impact them. They only value them on the court, field, or turf. This solidified my determination to do it, even if I had to do it alone."

Mynk was angry, but she was still anxious before actually taking that knee. "I was alone. There were no other Black players on my team. I was by myself doing it, with no support. It was hard; it was scary. The athletic director tried to talk me out of it, similar with what happened on the football team. I had teammates come up to me, trying to talk me out of it. It was rough."

Following Mynk's taking of a knee, the aftermath was hardly a festival of acceptance. "The school really tried to keep it quiet," she said. "They tried not to tell anyone, tried not to let it get out. But it got all the way to the president of the university and he did not respond well at all. I had to have meetings with the Title IX coordinator. I had to have meetings with the president and with the athletic director, because of how my team reacted to me. I remember my family and I sat down with the president, and we told him all these things I had been through and gone through on the team. At some point in the conversation, he brought up the fact that he couldn't possibly be racist because his daughter is dating a Black man. I pushed on through that and told him how my team attacked me. He was like, 'Well, that's just how the world is. You have to learn to defend yourself.' And I said, 'Well, first of all, I know how to defend myself, but I should not be put into an environment where I would have to. My team should not be allowed to react that way.' But I didn't receive any support from the president of the university, from my coaches, my teammates, none of that." During her sophomore season, in 2018, Mynk began taking a knee and did so for every single game for the rest of her lacrosse career at North Central.

At this point, Mynk does not see herself standing for the anthem ever again. "Not the way this country treats Black people, people of color, and marginalized groups. I refuse to stand for the anthem until this country stands for everyone."

Mynk is still aghast when she remembers some of the arguments that her teammates would throw at her. "They would say things like, 'I can't look my family in the eye and tell them that you're doing this, that you're taking a knee. My brother is in the military and he looks up to you.'" Mynk would respond, "'I don't know your family and I've never had a conversation with your brother before in my life. What are you talking about?'"

It was galling for her to have these teammates play the victim, as if this was something she was doing to *them*. "We had a team meeting," she recalled, still flabbergasted at the fragility on display. "This is probably one of the most ridiculous parts. The athletic directors were there. My coaches were there. The whole meeting was about them trying to get me to not take a knee." One player said of one of their teammates, "She's been crying all week because of what you're trying to do. Please don't take a knee. We'll go with you to BSA meetings. You're hurting our team. Your peaceful protest is hurting our team. You're not being a good leader. Can we link arms instead?"

As Mynk remembered, "They ganged up to get me not to do it and the coaches just stood there and let it happen! The athletic directors sat there and let them attack me for this hour-long team meeting. This one teammate had written me an open letter about her pain. It was ridiculous."

But Mynk wasn't entirely alone. Her mother and grandmother went to every game, home and away, and without fail took a knee with her. "There was this one game when this one dad was cursing at my mom. He was also yelling at me from the stands, calling me lazy, telling me to run faster. And it got to the point where he had to get kicked out of the stadium. The North Central parents were so bad that parents from other schools would cheer for me out of sympathy because of how awful they were."

If there is one lesson Mynk would want to pass on, it is the following: "There were just so many ways that when you're of color and you're in these white spaces, they try to silence you and try to make you feel like you're crazy or that you're the issue or that you're the problem, that it's your fault. I just want to say to anyone that's considering doing this or something like this that you're not the problem. You are not the issue. Don't let them gaslight you. Let your voice be heard. Let your story be heard, because it needs to happen. Reach out for support. I waited too late to reach out to people. There were days where I would leave practice in tears because of how they were treating me. I would try to talk to them and they would ignore me or roll their eyes at me. Don't let them gaslight you. What you're experiencing is real. What you're going through is valid. Reach out for help and continue fighting the good fight."

• • •

Trayviel (Tray) Boone took a knee at Dickinson State University in North Dakota, where he played football. Tray grew up in South Central Los Angeles. "Whatever you know about South Central is how it was. I've seen things, been around things, that other kids can only imagine, or only see on TV or hear it in music, or hear their friends talk about it. But I grew up with aspirations of doing something great. For me playing football, I felt like that was a fast track to be on a bigger platform and to be a positive influence."

Growing up, he was taught "to watch out, because you're always going to be a target. You being a young Black man in America, no matter what you do, no matter if you're a college graduate, you become a gang member in the eyes of many. You're a target." As for the police, they were regarded with fear. Police brutality was something Tray witnessed at a young age. As a result, "we were just afraid of the police. We don't deal with police, you know, that's just how the culture was."

Tray then left South Central to play football at Dickinson State—a culture shock, to put it mildly. "I was completely out of my element," he remembered. "Me being an inner-city kid, going all the way to North Dakota, going from a big city to such a small town, I really bit off more than I could chew. I was looking for a challenge, something different. Even dealing with the weather turned me upside down. As far as the people, they were very accepting. They were open, willing to get to know you and figure out where you're from. I loved Dickinson for that reason. They're real conservative, you know. They say that they don't like anyone bringing in no type of trouble."

Many of the other players on the team were from California,

and a lot of the stories of people getting killed by police hit home. The team started up their own club, called Open Talk. "It was basically just for anyone to come in and express themselves. We were already involved doing stuff for the community and the school and all of that, just so we could be better understood."

Before the players took a knee their nerves were very intense. "We were actually going to do it a couple of weeks before the day we actually did it, but it took some work. We started with trying to get the entire team to do it, but that didn't go the way we expected it, so it ended up being some of the guys and then the other half said no, but we didn't want the people in the community to see a divide in the team either. So us California kids decided to just go ahead and do it.

"When we did end up protesting at the game, we got negative feedback from the community. I could understand the reason why, but at the same time I just wished they would've understood where we were coming from. We tried our best to do what we did respectfully. Kaepernick had taken his knee, so we tried to figure out something where it was going to be okay with us and okay for the fans, the boosters, and just the entire community to see that we're actually trying to do it for the right cause, rather than bring trouble. When it came to taking a knee, for us it was just spreading awareness. We felt like it was our opportunity to do it here, in North Dakota."

Tre Nowaczynski took a knee as a football player at Macalester College in St. Paul, Minnesota. Like Colin Kaepernick, Tre is from Milwaukee, Wisconsin, and is a "transracial adoptee." He said, "Growing up in white spaces, white schools, with a white family, I was pretty aware of race as a concept very early," he said. "I definitely experienced some minor differential treatment than some of my peers. It wasn't something that I was entirely aware of until probably middle school or high school. I think that's when things started to become a little bit more apparent."

Racism and violence hit Tre hard in high school when "I had a friend, pretty close to me, who died at the hands of community members. They held him under citizen's arrest and they ended up choking him to death. There was a lot of public conversation about why it happened, like, if it was justified or not. That was a pretty shocking realization—that not only was he killed but that the terms of the discussion were about whether he deserved to die. I think somewhere in that time frame, slightly after, there was national news surrounding Trayvon Martin's death, and I think that sparked my real engrossment in just exactly what kinds of things were going on at the hands of the police."

Macalester College—my alma mater as well—was a contradictory place for Tre. "I was really excited about their multicultural emphasis and the rigor of their academic programs in general. I think being an athlete there carried a different responsibility, just because it is a school that is not focused on athletics, and I think that allowed for a lot of growth outside of some of those traditionally masculine spaces," he said. "But I will say that as they promote multicultural diversity, I was still one of the very few African American males that were on campus at any time. I think that was something that we had a lot of conversation about continuously. I mean, colleges all over the country are still grappling with those issues as they become more diverse, but still don't have access to low-income Black families or students who are ready and eager to go to schools like that. The longer I stayed at Macalester, the more I felt that and the more that I felt like I was carrying the burden of my community through sports, through my work in the classroom, all of that."

The summer before Tre's senior year, St. Paul's Philando Castile was killed by police. The shock and outrage that emerged from the Twin Cities, coupled with Kaepernick first protesting that August, compelled Tre to act. "Actually, one of my teammates suggested that we do it, but he wanted to do it in solidarity, together. So at that time, there were probably three or four Black men on the team, and two of us decided that we wanted to take a knee and two of our teammates chose to kneel with us, but we were the only four out of a team of sixty-some-odd guys."

Tre believes that there were people on the team who felt like they shouldn't be doing it, "but I was a captain at that point and nobody was really trying to stand in my way. I think something to note was that my co-captain—he was a ROTC guy, so he's serving in the military now—he didn't kneel, but he told me, in private conversations, that he was in full support of what we were doing, and I think that also gave me a lot of encouragement to continue."

While the team was largely supportive, many of the parents of players were not. Also, when they would be at away games, they were "identified as the kneelers and had to hear generic racial slurs and comments. I think even a coach at one point said something to me while I was on the field."

Tre said that it "felt good to be able to take some kind of

stand beyond the academic and activist-involved work that some of us were doing." He also wrote an editorial about kneeling for the school newspaper, because while their actions were creating a lot of discussion in other spaces, there was a "lack of response" on campus. "Our intention was to get people to ask us, 'Okay, so why are you doing this? What are things we can do individually or as a community?' I honestly was kind of looking for some punitive action to take place, or somebody to say, 'No, you can't do this,' or for more people to join, but it didn't ever feel that way." The article did lead to sitting down with the school athletic director to talk about diversity and his experience as an athlete of color in the department.

One reason the kneeling may not have sparked that discussion is that the football program at the liberal-leaning Division III school is not your typical program. "The Macalester football program brands itself as kind of a more progressive program in the country," Tre said. This is a school more likely to draw students to a protest rally than a football game. In fact, the Macalester community would have been shocked if no one had knelt.

St. Michael's College is a small, predominantly white liberal arts college of sixteen hundred undergraduates in Colchester, Vermont, right near what residents call "the People's Republic of Burlington." In 2017 basketball players and coaching staff took a knee—and the response was life changing for the participants involved. Long Island, New York, native Winston Jones was a forward on that team. Culture shock aside, his experience was very positive. "I think the main thing that stuck out for me, besides being a scholarship player and getting tested to play college basketball, was how interested the school was in who I was as a person before anything basketball-wise came up, and how adamant they were about having me be part of their program. My dad always tells me that when it comes to going anywhere, be it a job, playing basketball, or a relationship, you need to go where you're valued and where you're wanted."

His coach Joshua Meyer believed in teaching social justice through coaching. Meyer said, "I got my graduate degree in education, so I developed a kind of educator's philosophy and tried to incorporate that as much as possible into my coaching pedagogy and what we were trying to do. I had a desire to get back into college coaching and I had been to Burlington, Vermont, and thought it was a really nice place. We had just started our family and we thought it'd be a good place for us to move to, so we gave it a shot."

Winston was first aware that police brutality was something he would have to reckon with when his parents sat him down and gave him "the talk." "I think I can speak for a lot of African American youth and people of color with this," he said. "You know how parents used to give their kids the 'sex talk'? Usually in houses like mine, you had the 'racism talk,' and afterwards the 'cop talk.' You kind of see that as early as kindergarten. Like going to the store and being told, 'Don't put your hands in your pockets,' or 'Don't touch a lot of stuff in the store,' you know, and 'Give everybody a firm handshake,' and being coached on how to be perceived as 'safe.' And that was, like, the introduction to understanding the complex, systematic establishment of racism in this country and in the world."

Coach Meyer had his own set of experiences that influenced his actions. "I have a multiracial family," he said. "My partner is a Black woman; we are raising two Black daughters in this world and I am a white man, so I have quite a bit of privilege. Our experiences on a daily basis are really different. The air we breathe is different. The system that exhausts them and that questions their self-worth *works* for me. And that's something that we're navigating on a daily basis. My partner and I have been having conversations around that even before we had kids. But being part of diverse sports teams at an early age where I got to be teammates with people from very different backgrounds and different races, I really started to see the privilege that I had as a white person. I was able to get a sense of how we live in very different worlds based on our skin color. Now I see how racism impacts my daughters and my partner and the toll that it takes on them with microaggressions, feelings about self-worth, mental health, and the work that we have to do to really let our kids know how valued they are and how important they are and how beautiful they are. I think that really just connected with my experiences as a coach and helped me understand and create a space for our student-athletes and have our team be a place where they were seen, heard, valued, and cared for—not just as basketball players, but as people, as human beings."

The motivation for Winston to take a knee started with Colin Kaepernick. "I didn't really think much of it when he did it initially, but what turned the spark in me was the reaction from others and how angry and heated and disgusted people were by it. Initially I couldn't quite grasp why people thought it was so blasphemous." This reaction compelled Winston to want to use his platform to provoke "uncomfortable discussions."

"Having been an athlete my whole life, I know that people

have perceptions of athletes as being disconnected, especially as college athletes. I thought about how I was at St. Mike's, which is over 90 percent Caucasian, and the majority of our team are Black players, and I was thinking, 'You know what? I'm going to show people that I'm not just here to win games, I'm not just here to play basketball and make the alumni donors happy.' I need people to understand that I am Winston, with or without the purple and white across my chest, and if you want Winston here, you have to have all of Winston, not just when he's getting rebounds or making free throws."

Before taking a knee, the team had a locker-room discussion to make sure that players who weren't on board at least understood why coaches and some teammates felt compelled to act. As Winston recalled, "It was awkward at first because no one wants to sound offensive or angry or extra self-righteous or disturb the feng shui of the team. You're used to locker-room talk being about video games or seeing this highlight or stuff going on back home, so when you have real conversations, it's awkward at first and uneasy, but I thought it was important to ask everyone—not necessarily so much about whether they would or wouldn't kneel, but what they valued, and the big ones that came up for our team were family, integrity, and camaraderie. A lot of us came from different backgrounds and have very different stories, and a lot of us really got a chance to learn about each other on a deeper level. Like, what's your 'why'? What pushes you to get up every day and do the same routine? I think once we found out all of our 'whys' and our values, it made our conversation a little bit easier."

As a coach, Joshua Meyer did not want to dictate anything that he felt his team had to do. Instead he said, "We just tried to create a student-centered space that was about them and their growth and their voice. Where they would share their voice, where people were empowered, and I think once you establish that type of space, people can do some really amazing things through sport."

The decision to take a knee had been made. It would start against their Division I opponent University of Vermont, and as nervous as the players and coaches may have been, no one expected what would follow.

Winston remembered, "I can see that UVM game so vividly in my head, and it's funny because when we first did it, we thought we'd just make our statement and be done with it. We knew fans were going to be out there and the season was just getting under way. It was the game where we'd really see how progressive people actually were. Everyone could talk a big game, everyone could sound nice or smile in your face, but we would see how supportive people were when athletes weren't being the athletes that they might want to see."

As the anthem started, some players and coaches at St. Mike's took that knee. As Winston described it, "I mean, boy! I expected some backlash, but there was booing, racial slurs, stuff thrown on the court. People in the stands were getting kicked. Even the security guards were like, 'Yeah, this is too much.' But then I also heard some cheers, some clapping, a lot of protection as well, especially from Coach Meyer's wife. She was one of the main people who stood up right away and was almost trying to shield us like we were her kids, like she had thirteen sons on that court and was like, 'Do not touch my babies!' And I had kept my head down initially, but I decided they needed to see my face, so I lifted my head and told everyone else to do the same. We were going to stand firm and look straight ahead. Seeing and hearing it all and being in that moment just put a spark in me, a sense of pride in who I was because I understood that that was what people meant by leaving a legacy behind."

Coach Meyer had a similar description of the UVM game. "It was a very racist environment. People were yelling all types of things at the team, and it was charged and scary. My partner and my two daughters were behind the bench, and people were running up to the bench and yelling things at the team. We were definitely worried about their safety. There were people trying to stand up for us as well, and they said things to the people shouting at the team, but it was still extremely charged. Vermont is perceived as this really liberal, progressive state, and it was anything but liberal and progressive at that game. It was blatantly racist, and no one really did anything to stop it. It's a big game every year because it's two local colleges and it's an exhibition game, so it's a packed gym with three or four thousand people. You have leaders in the community from each college there, you have UVM leadership from the school, and no one did anything to stop it. It was able to play itself out and people were yelling at us to stand up. People were also yelling things that were a lot worse than that. It was really difficult to go through that and we were worried about the guys and how they were feeling. When people were running up to the bench after we protested, no one really did anything to stop that either. I think someone could have easily gotten on the microphone and addressed it, but racism was really allowed to just do what it wanted to do on that day. As for my wife, someone came up to the bench and she was trying to both protect her family and shield the team from harm, and she was verbally assaulted and was asked to sit down. She works at UVM, so it was a really difficult experience for her, being part of an institution that preaches these liberal values and wasn't living up to them. So that was really disheartening for her and for us as a family."

There were people in the community who supported what the team did, but from an institutional standpoint, neither UVM nor St. Michael's offered the team even a modicum of support. "There was a lot of harm done because of how UVM handled it," said Coach Meyer. "And then on the St. Michael's side, there were people in the community who supported us, but from an institutional standpoint, they did not support us. Our president released a statement that was not supportive. So we definitely felt like we were on an island. In our community there were some media responses, like a local ESPN radio affiliate that called our actions 'performative' with no real understanding of all that had gone into what the team did. So much went into it beforehand in terms of conversation and the work that we had been doing, and then so much work was done afterwards to educate and help people understand and try to bring people together and heal the community. We definitely had people who supported us too, but this was well before it was popular to take a knee."

What may have made this instance particularly threatening was that white coaches took a knee along with the players. "I think that the way we did it and what it represented was very scary for people. It was a threat to systems. The team was really protesting systemic racism but also all forms of oppression, and I think that systems and whiteness don't appreciate it when they see that. These current models of coaching and teams are very authoritative and based in white supremacy, and when a team does what we did, protesting against racism, it's really protesting against all systems, including the NCAA, which is based on these very authoritative models that control student-athletes of color, controlling Black and Brown bodies. When those systems are challenged—and we're talking about systems that are living, breathing things—they don't like it. People don't like it. People in positions of power, coaches who have authoritative frameworks and philosophies—it throws everything for a loop, and ultimately, you're talking about a framework that could challenge the NCAA too. If you want a team to go out to midfield during the Fiesta Bowl and decide not to play, you have to create cultures and team dynamics where student-athletes' voices are heard and where they're empowered, where it's not an authoritative, hierarchical structure. We really tried to do that, and I think some of these things were a reflection of what we were doing and of the really special student-athletes that we had who do have a voice. They just need a space where their voices can be heard. And they need to feel like they can be their true selves."

St. Mike's lost the game, but Winston said, "No one even talked about the score or anything like that. I think we can see that the impact this made for many years to come is pretty substantial. People I'd never spoken to before on campus were now coming up to me and saying, 'Thank you,' 'I appreciate you speaking up,' 'You showed me something different,' 'I learned from you.' I think a lot of the time people are either too prideful to say that they're wrong and learn or too scared to say, 'I want to learn.' And so I look at myself like, 'I'll take the bullet initially if it's going to lead to someone else having shelter or protection.' Right now, it's almost easy or trendy or cool to be someone who stands up for social justice. Which is great! I'm glad it's seen as cool now for people to be able to do it and jump in. But it's possible because there was a first group to get the backlash, to not be cool or trendy or comfortable."

For the rest of the season, some schools refused to play the national anthem if St. Mike's was coming to town. Winston said, "It made me laugh, thinking, 'Y'all are that scared, huh?' For me, at least they recognized what we were doing, and they knew what the reaction would be if we did it. That gave me all the power I needed, so I was like, 'Okay, it wouldn't matter if you played the anthem or not if you knew that the reaction was going to be hugs and kisses. But you know that playing it is going to cause some disruption.' So that let me know right then and there, from that moment on, that we did the right thing. We opened people's eyes greatly. People were in a slumber, and now the nightmare was starting, but for a good reason. And it needed to happen. So, for me, it wasn't necessarily outright support, but I knew people were watching and I knew people were talking, and I knew that that was going to get the ball rolling in a direction it needed to go."

Winston believes that taking that knee didn't so much "change" his life as "reinvigorate" it. "Taking that action repurposed how I live. I say that because it made me want to take on things that made me uncomfortable. It showed me the importance and power that I possess in my voice, and how much potential as a leader I actually have. It gave me my 'why,' my motivation for doing things, and it showed me that people listen. Out of a hundred people, I know one person is going to hear me. And that one person may now have the power to influence a hundred people, or a thousand, or even just one other person. But nothing in life is going to start by being silent. I think people need to understand that."

As for Coach Meyer, today he is no longer working at St. Michael's, having left the school in 2019. He said, "My first two years were winning seasons. The next four weren't winning seasons. My best moments were when we were doing social justice work and when we were doing retreats that really brought us together as a team and allowed the student-athletes to unpack their identities and talk about their different experiences. The educational piece and the social justice piece were what I was most passionate about. I always saw myself as an educator. That's why I loved basketball. It's really difficult to exist in a world where college sports are not educational; they're a business. It has more to do with winning and making money than anything else. If you're someone who's an educator, who really believes in empowering student-athletes, I think once you're awake and you see these things, you understand the world you exist in and it loses its soul for you. It's not where you want to be. It definitely lost its soul for me. I found myself on a daily basis having to fight a battle where I didn't care how many games we won. I wanted the student-athletes to have a really impactful and transformative learning experience. I wanted them to be seen and heard. And I wanted to go against the system and do everything I could to work against the system. It's hard to do that. It's exhausting. I've transitioned to education and practicing restorative justice work in Burlington, Vermont, in K–12 schools in our district."

I ask Coach Meyer how one can be a "social-justice-oriented

coach." He said, "It can't be performative; it has to be real. That comes back to changing the model of coaching and how coaches are trained. Part of that training includes self-work, especially for white coaches like me. We have to understand the privilege that we have as white people and white men. We have to truly understand the experiences of others, what student-athletes of color have experienced in their lives and what they're experiencing at primarily white institutions, and how important it is to do that work. You can't just show up one day and say, 'I'm going to coach for social justice.' You have to do deep work. You have to read. You have to listen to the experiences of people who have been marginalized. I think that takes systemic transformation. We need to change the system of college sports and the model of coaching. That starts at the highest level of college basketball, but it trickles down. We see it in youth sports. We see it at all levels of college basketball where coaches feel that they have to win basketball games and that's the priority, and we have to move away from that model to one where education is the priority. The growth of our student-athletes and preparing them for life after college is the most important thing. There's a lot of change that's necessary."

Cherokee Washington played volleyball at Whitman College in Walla Walla, Washington. "I grew up in California. I'm from L.A. I was born and went to school in Santa Monica," she said. "I have a loving family, but I've been in a very white, homogenous space as an African American child. So that instilled in me from the get-go, as a young kid, a different way of looking at things from my peers. I come from a family of athletes. I have a little brother who's also an athlete. My mom's a personal trainer. She also played volleyball in college. My dad ran track. And he's a speed coach, right now, for NFL Combine prospects. So sports is in the family."

When Cherokee was older, her parents told her stories about getting profiled by police when walking her in her stroller. "Those stories stuck," she remembered.

Cherokee went to a middle school that was predominantly white, but the change in her life when she started to look at the world in a different manner was her senior year of high school, when Trayvon Martin was killed. "When Trayvon Martin got shot, that was when my world opened up. I was like, 'Holy shit, this is not okay.' I was like, 'All right, I gotta somehow add to solving this problem.'"

After high school, Cherokee chose to attend Whitman College. "It's a very white town, super tiny," she said. "There's a little bit of diversity, but on the outskirts. It's a weird place. I didn't think in a million years I'd end up there. A lot of people from Portland and Seattle, Northern California, a lot of white kids, which isn't a problem, but it lends to having one particular experience and having a staff of professors and people on campus who cater to a certain group, even if inadvertently."

Cherokee believes that she was far more socially aware than her fellow students because she was schooled in activism as well as diversity and inclusion before matriculating at Whitman. "By the time I got to Whitman, I wasn't playing any games. I got really heavily involved in student government and a couple of groups that did social justice work. And then being an athlete myself, I was always speaking up about different issues. I was really lucky to be a student-athlete and be friends with so many students of color who also happened to be student-athletes. I think my volleyball team was probably the most diverse of all the teams, and there were only twelve or thirteen of us. We were definitely way more diverse than any brochure I ever saw at Whitman, which is ridiculous. But it's a great school and I received a phenomenal education. I went into the rhetoric department, and that's where a lot of students of color and students from marginalized backgrounds happened to congregate too, so I was lucky to have professors who were supporting me as well. But at times it was tough, to say the least."

Cherokee was pushed to take a knee because "I think I was just fed up with the world. As a Black woman, I was in this space of an 'Angry Black Woman' kind of personality. Trump was doing his thing and I was in college and I was pissed off with my campus and the president of the school wasn't doing anything about police brutality experienced by students. I had gone to her with different issues and I was in student government by then, so I was becoming privy to issues on campus that made me even more upset. Things weren't moving and I was just pissed."

Cherokee was also listening to Tupac and Kendrick Lamar, learning about John Carlos and Tommie Smith and looking for "a silent or a physical protest that was nonviolent." Enter Kaepernick. "The moment Kaepernick knelt, I thought, 'Everybody needs to be doing this.' So I talked to my teammates before I did it. I said, 'Hey, guys, I know that you know that I'm very involved in activism as an athlete, but I want to make sure that you are comfortable with me kneeling. I'm going to do it anyway, but if anyone has an issue, I'm happy to talk to them about it.'" Her coaches did not quite understand where she was coming from, but they said, "Okay, I guess you can do your thing."

Then Cherokee wrote a letter to the entire Whitman community that said, "I'm kneeling. If anyone wants to join me, feel free."

That call was not heeded, and Cherokee was alone in taking a knee—but that didn't stop her teammates from supporting her. "I'm really lucky to have had a team of friends that I'm still best friends with today, where we all support each other 100 percent, even if we don't fully agree with something someone is doing. They without hesitation said, 'Do your thing. We totally understand. We're not necessarily kneeling with you, but we're there with you, in spirit and physically on the court.'"

She also found full support from her athletic director and her allies in student government. And then it had a ripple effect as most of the soccer team took a knee. Other than some snarky comments, Cherokee was not attacked on campus, although emails came from the community to both her and the school demanding that she be disciplined. "I was like, really? Disciplined? We can have a conversation, people."

Cherokee observes that her support came just about entirely from female athletes. "I was hoping that the men's basketball team would kneel with me," she said, "because most of my friends are from that team and are African American as well. I wasn't expecting them to, necessarily, but it was interesting to see that women were supporting me a little bit more than men. I don't know why that was the case, but I do know that as women, we have different things that we have to face versus men, because men are always going to be—whether they are Black, Asian, Hispanic—above us in the social food chain. I think that rallied us together a little bit differently."

Cherokee said that, following the protests of 2020, she feels a sense of vindication about her experience taking a knee. She said, "My coach actually called me from college the other day. It was kind of a three-part apology. First, he texted me: 'Checking in on you. How are you doing? I hope you're okay. I just want to take the time to acknowledge that I didn't navigate your kneeling back in college the right way.' Then he called me a couple of days later and said, 'I want to make sure we Face-Time and I give you a proper apology' for handling things the way he did and putting a cap on my protest and therefore putting a cap on my identity, my community, and what Kaepernick was trying to do. I don't know if I can ever quite forgive him because they put policies in place after I did it where we weren't allowed to do any kind of protesting, or anything at all. It's been a weird roundabout. I feel a little bit vindicated by the personal pieces that are being put together back in my life, but on a grander scale I do think this is definitely a movement that is helping other people affirm and believe what we're going through, as people of color, especially Black people. We're moving in the right direction, where we understand this is happening, but some white people are now on our side and are saying, 'We also can't let this happen.' I think George Floyd's murder opened the eyes of America."

Keyonna Morrow played volleyball at West Virginia Tech. She grew up in Indiana, living with her mother, and also in "very rural" Kentucky with her father.

Growing up was not easy for Keyonna. "There would be white people that would call me the Oreo—Black on the outside, white on the inside—and I would think to myself, 'You probably shouldn't be saying that. But I'm going to leave it alone because if I say something, then I'm the angry Black girl and we *still* have a problem.'"

West Virginia Tech was an entirely new experience for her after being raised in a rural environment. "There were tons of international students," she said. "It was an engineering school and technically the school is considered to be low-level athletics. So the student-athletes that are there are good at their sport, but they're also really smart."

During Keyonna's junior year, she made some history by helping to launch the school's first Black Student Union. "Keep in mind, we're in deep West Virginia," she said. "There are not very many Black people and the ones that are there are not representative of the rest of us, so when we started BSU, we felt like it was necessary, because everybody else had a cultural organization that was for them. We didn't think it would be a problem to start a Black Student Union when there's an African Culture Association, Brazilian Culture Association, and other groups. But when we tried to start our BSU, the school told us that it sounded exclusionary. I'm not sure how they got to that but they said to us, 'It sounds like you're only inviting Black people.' And our response was always, 'Okay, so if I'm not a biology major, am I going to go to biology club?' It's not us saying you have to Black to be in here, but this is a safe space created for the Black students and it turns out that we created it at the perfect time."

Keyonna was pushed to take a knee because "look, I'm a nice person, but when it comes to certain things, I'm an ass. This happened to be one of them. People taking a knee was in the news, and I would hear people on campus saying things like, 'They're sheep' and 'just followers.' I'm would hit them back with, 'That's like saying, if you're getting a driver's license at sixteen, you're just being a sheep. You want to drive? You get a license. Well, I want justice.' One of my biggest pet peeves is people stepping into other people's business. If it is not directly affecting you or your family, why are you worried about it? It just started to piss me off. So that morning, the morning of the game, I woke up and I'm on Facebook. I'm reading more and more ignorant comments and I'm thinking, 'You know what? I'm going to do this because I need people to understand this is not about you.' It's kind of like how kids throw a tantrum. They don't actually want to throw themselves on the ground. They want you to hear what they have to say or try to help them get their point across. I'm not saying we were throwing a temper tantrum, but it's not about the flag. If you say it is, that just means you're not listening. So I messaged a bunch of people in the BSU group and also people that were outside of the BSU group and everyone said, 'Yeah, let's do it!' Sure enough, the photos that made the papers didn't show the whole picture: they showed us on the field but didn't show all of the people taking a knee in the stands, showing the world that this was not just about the athletes."

Keyonna's coach was out on maternity leave but was still keeping track of what was happening. Keyonna said that her coach called her to her house a few days later and told her that her taking a knee "would haunt me for the rest of my days. I said back, 'I don't think it's going to haunt me because I'm proud of it.' I think of haunting as something that's wearing on you, something bad that you're not proud of that you want to get away from. I don't want to get away from it. I tell people all the time, 'Google me!' No, it definitely doesn't haunt me. As for my coach, she was pissed because she felt like we were still thinking about it during the game and that's why we lost. No. We lost because we lost."

As far as Keyonna's team, there was only one member who was furious about it because her family was in the armed forces. "She felt like it was disrespectful to the military—which a lot of people say, and I cannot, for the life of me, understand that." Many teammates were international, "so they said, 'I don't care. It's not my flag anyway, so I couldn't care less.'"

One teammate wanted to sit down and really discuss it. It ended with her saying, "I wouldn't have done it, but I understand why you did. I never would have thought of any of that. I never would have even looked at it from a different perspective, if you and I hadn't had this conversation."

Ian Troost was a kicker at the University of Pittsburgh and knelt during the national anthem in the fall of 2017. "For me being a white male from New Hampshire, I was tone-deaf to a lot of what's going on in this country," he remembered. "I've learned that what people of color are subjected to in this country, in terms of systemic racism, stemming all the way from housing to dealing with police on an everyday basis to just everyday interactions, is above and beyond what is fair and just."

Growing up in an area "hovering right around a 94–95 percent white population," Ian was raised with the idea that "racism is just the Ku Klux Klan, racial slurs, and hate crimes." Beyond that the thinking was, "Slavery was abolished over 150 years ago, so how is the United States still racist? That's kind of the mind-set I grew up in. Going to a public school in a very white state, I was given a very whitewashed education, and there's no way to challenge that in a state like New Hampshire."

It took moving to Pittsburgh to kick for the football team and having two Black roommates to change Ian's thinking. "Being in a city where there is a much higher population of Black people, people of color, and minority groups, you need to understand the intricacies and nuances of not just blatant racism but subtle racism. Just everything that I never really got growing up."

He started talking more to his roommates, Dontez Ford and Reggie Mitchell, which had a great effect on how he started seeing the world. "I remember Dontez was from McKees Rocks and we were having a conversation around midnight. I told them a story about growing up in Portsmouth, and our relationship with police. Dontez said in response, 'Yeah, I remember being arrested when I was a young teenager, around thirteen, because I fit the description of a twenty-one-year-old Black male.' I said, 'No way, that's crazy.' He said, 'Yeah, they arrested me.' I asked, 'Did you tell them you weren't that person?' He said, 'Of course I told them I wasn't that person. I'm not an idiot. But they said no, you fit the description. You are this person.' And at that moment, it clicked for me. That was the 'holy shit' moment for me. The police just didn't care that it wasn't the right person and that he was a thirteen-year-old boy."

Then, when Colin Kaepernick started kneeling, Ian and his roommates had another late-night back-and-forth. "We would have these conversations about it and I remember them being interested in kneeling, but they thought, 'I definitely wouldn't be allowed to do that.'"

The next year Donald Trump called Colin Kaepernick and

other kneeling athletes "sons of bitches," and that "threw it right back into the spotlight."

NFL players then began protesting again. "Kenny Stills and a few other players, obviously Eric Reid, started to really step it up. It got me remembering Dontez and Reggie saying, 'Hey, we don't think we'd be allowed to kneel,' the year prior. I wondered, 'Are players allowed to kneel on our team?' My thought process jumped to how I could be an ally."

Ian thought that if there were players that were going to kneel for the anthem, "I wanted to kneel with them. I wanted to hopefully show that this wasn't just a protest for people of color and Black people. So then that kind of turned into people pressing me: 'Why do you want to kneel?' 'Can you explain why you want to kneel?' 'Do you understand why you're kneeling?' It kind of snowballed into this whole thing with the athletic department and coaches putting me under a microscope about it. So ultimately, I met with a lot of different people in the administration. I met with friends of mine. I really wanted to make sure that I wasn't hijacking the movement to make it about me, a white third-string kicker. Ultimately that became a big argument against me from other people. I thought it would be powerful to show that, hey, I'm doing this with my teammates. Hopefully in support of them. I remember having a lot of conversations with Dontez and Reggie and them being like, 'Hey, man, if we were still on the team [they were seniors the year prior], we would 100 percent be doing it.' That kind of was a driving force."

Before that first game when Ian knelt, "only my teammates and coaches knew. No one really caught wind of it. I wasn't trying to do this for attention. Obviously, the ultimate goal was to create conversation about why a white person would be kneeling during the national anthem and creating hopefully positive conversation."

Ian saw those kinds of dialogues as key to racial equity because those were exactly the kinds of conversations he got into with Dontez and Reggie. "In 2014, I would get into screaming matches with my best friend from New Hampshire. I had no idea and I didn't want to listen to my friends who were correct about it all, because I was just regurgitating stuff that I learned growing up, like 'Why not just listen to police officers? Then nothing bad would happen.' That's what I and so many people were taught growing up. Then conversations with Dontez and Reggie and little conversations throughout my college career led me to have an antiracist consciousness, so ultimately, I wanted to create dialogue on and off campus with my friends and my family that would lead to a deeper understanding of the issues. That's why I took a knee. But it did lead to a lot of backlash."

The backlash did not start until after the second game when Ian knelt. It started with "random people sending me messages on social media. People telling me to kill myself. . . ."

Ian believes that if he had been Black or a person of color, the backlash would have been far worse. "I just had people telling me that I hate America and that I was a 'liberal Nazi,'" he remembered. "I had support from friends, which was great, but a lot of teammates wouldn't look me in the eye. They wouldn't even speak to me. A few really went out of their way to make things kind of hellish for me. One day I came in for practice and I had Gatorade dumped all over my shoulder pads. This was at six a.m. I remember just shrugging it off; I didn't want to make a scene with any of the coaches or anything. My whole goal was to remain low-key and try to prove to the coaches that I wasn't a distraction, so I didn't want to bother anyone with it. Then after practice, I went to my locker and someone had dumped juice all over my clothes."

The coaches got wind of this and instead of trying to figure out who would mess with his uniform and clothes, they turned on Ian for being "a distraction." Ian went from being friends with some players to "they wouldn't even speak to me or they'd give me dirty looks or be really short with me. Some coaches wouldn't even look me in the eye unless there was an opportunity to scream at me."

A few of the coaches were still civil, but Ian would find himself "randomly" drug tested a great deal more than his peers. It was that kind of scene. "I had a few meetings with people in the athletic administration who made it clear that I was costing the University of Pittsburgh money."

As bad as it was, Ian realized that "as a white person, I have the privilege to be able to turn it off. Obviously, it was extremely exhausting, dealing with that on a day-to-day basis, nervous on campus that someone was going to sucker punch me, constantly feeling like I was under a microscope. I know, obviously, I brought it upon myself, but I also had had the ability as a white person to take a step back away from it, and that's a privilege, whereas a person of color is constantly dealing with racism in every nuance of their lives. Colin Kaepernick chose to start this movement and bring it to light: the act of kneeling for the anthem, it affects his life every single day. He doesn't have a job; he's blackballed by the NFL. To me, ultimately, people have forgotten that I did it. I'm proud of the conversations it led to, but it's privilege that I don't have to deal with the fallout every day anymore."

Jordan Oster played women's basketball at Pacific University, where she put up a fist during the national anthem. Oster grew up in Santa Clarita, California, an upper-middle-class, conservative town. "I didn't really know anything about race or racial injustice until I started college. So that was never at the forefront of my mind when I was growing up."

After high school, Jordan went to a community college for two years and played basketball there. That was the first time she was around a significant number of people of color and was introduced to other people's experiences.

Jordan started to question everything she had been taught after Michael Brown was killed. Ferguson exploded, and the powers that be decided to not even prosecute Officer Darren Wilson for Brown's death. "That's what did it for me and what really woke me up. I think a similar thing is happening right now for a lot of people. They are being forced to confront the reality that society is set up in a way that puts specific groups at a disadvantage and a lot of people aren't comfortable with it. But I never thought that we would see this many people wake up all at once. It's a really stressful and scary time and you feel helpless, but that's been one good thing that I've seen. A lot of people that I never thought would speak up have been speaking up."

Oster felt compelled to raise her fist not only after seeing Kaepernick take a knee but also after observing the reactions to his protest and listening to his explanation as to why he was doing it. "It was after the 2016 election," she said. "I felt like if I didn't do it, I would be doing myself and everyone else a disservice. It didn't feel right not to do something, because I was surrounded by a lot of white liberals. Everyone in that kind of climate expresses their negative feelings about Trump, but they didn't have this deep fear or disgust about it. It was just this surface-level thing and they didn't understand."

Jordan went to her coach and assumed there would be a level of understanding about why she wanted to take a knee because they were both members of the LGBTQ community. But that wasn't the case. "She just basically told me that if I wanted to do it, I needed to get the whole team to do it with me because it had to be a team thing. And she knew that the whole team wouldn't do it with me. I was basically stuck and I said, 'Can I at least put a fist up?' And she said, 'Yeah.' But I wish I would've taken a knee. I feel like by raising a fist, I compromised on something that I felt so strongly about because I was uncomfortable with the idea of disappointing my coach and not being a team player, not putting my team first, and so I compromised. If I were in that situation again, that definitely wouldn't be the case because this is something that I feel so strongly about, and as time has passed, I feel even stronger. I don't think I did the movement justice by compromising. If it would've been a fist from the beginning . . . if I had come to her and said I want to put a fist up, and she agreed, I think that would've been fine. But just the mere fact that I compromised on it, that's my regret. I wish I would've stood a little stronger on that."

Fortunately, Jordan's teammates were largely supportive in their comments to her. "A lot of them didn't understand, but they weren't ever negative about it. There were some team-mates that definitely understood. They just didn't feel comfortable joining me, but the majority of them didn't really understand what was going on. I love my team. My best friends were on my basketball team. They just weren't involved in any of the struggles that were taking place. I had a couple of professors too, and they were definitely supportive and validated my choice."

Jordan has often been asked, "As a white person, why did you enter this space and raise your fist?" She said, "I always respond similarly, just trying to explain the concept of whiteness and how it is our responsibility to not just be 'nonracist' but to be actively antiracist, because the way that the system is set up, if we go through our whole lives not bothering anyone and doing the right thing, we're still participating in a racist system, so our actions in turn reinforce that racist system. You have to be so conscious of your actions. You have to be intentional with what you're doing, or else you're no better than anyone else that's not putting in any effort to make the world better, because we're just feeding into the system. I point people to a book by Michael Eric Dyson, *Tears We Cannot Stop: A Sermon to White America*. That book really helped me out. Ever since the killing of George Floyd, a lot of my white friends have been asking me for resources and I always point them to that book. Always. It was so helpful to me to grapple with whiteness and our responsibility as white people to be better. Because if we're not actively trying to be better, we're just, by default, part of the problem."

•   •   •

Max Nagle was a basketball player at Hollins University, in Roanoke, Virginia. A trans man who played on the women's team at Hollins, Max grew up in northern Virginia, where he attended "the most diverse high school in the area, which in hindsight I'm really thankful for. I think it exposed me to a lot more that I wouldn't have gotten at a whiter school."

This led Max to being aware of "more marginalized groups and who was getting oppressed in the country. It led to me just giving a shit about that." When in college he learned the politics around issues like racial profiling, it gave him the facts to go with his instincts that the world was operating in a manner neither fair nor balanced. And when Kaepernick started taking a knee, Max thought that "he shouldn't be the only one doing this. There's no reason why I shouldn't be doing it as well."

At a school like Hollins, the debates are less about whether police brutality is worth protesting and more along the lines of, as Max remembered, "how to be a proper feminist and who's the most woke. It's a pretty left-leaning liberal arts college." That said, the team traveled to Trump country in the southern part of Virginia, and Max thought, "I would be safer doing it than some of my teammates, who were not white."

I asked Max if he told his team beforehand. He said, "When I got to school in the fall, I talked to the Black teammate I was closest with and told her that I was thinking of doing it, and she . . . I don't know if she was thinking of doing it before then, but she seemed totally on board with the idea. So we had a 'Cool, we're going to do this, because this country is really fucked up' moment. Then, closer to the season, when we actually started practicing, another Black teammate who I didn't know as well said that she was going to do it also. She announced it to the team and the coach said, 'And that's that. We're not going to argue about it.'

Max learned the lesson that courage is contagious. "I think I realized that doing something that you might not consider to be such a big deal can actually make a bigger difference. We were the first team at Hollins that did it that year. After that, someone on the soccer team did it, and then someone on the lacrosse team did it. Once we started doing it, it spread. I did it through the end of my junior season and only stopped because I stopped playing before senior year when I started testosterone. No one really did it as consistently as us, though. It confused me, because it was such an easy thing to do. We were the only ones doing it repeatedly no matter where we were."

Max also sees a connection between taking a knee, his aspiration to be a sportswriter, and coming to terms with being trans. "I'm transgender, but my whiteness is going to protect me over most anything else in a lot of scenarios. So I then have the ability to write about stuff and share my story and share other stories that might not get as much backlash. It's the same thing as I said with taking a knee in the first place. I'm probably safer in doing it because I'm white. I remember thinking that I wished more white teammates would take a knee, if for no other reason than it would take the weight off the Black players."

Maya McCann played soccer at Smith College. As a white person, Maya "grew up in Springfield, Massachusetts, in a pretty economically depressed area: a mostly Latino and Black community. We grew up having kitchen-table conversations about power, privilege, and equity. I went to public school in Spring-field, where my dad was a teacher and then a principal, and my mom worked at Springfield College. So they were dedicated to the community and made sure that as we grew up we were aware of who we were. We talked about what it meant to be white and middle-class in a community where most of our peers were not white or middle-class."

Maya appreciated that Smith was an all-women's school. "There's a uniqueness about seeing yourself represented in all the positions of power and having gender be at the forefront of conversation. But in addition to that, I think that Smith was a terrific community where people were passionate about not only academics but social justice issues. Being an athlete was great. DIII is different than others. They definitely cared about us having really strong academic, extracurricular, and athletic balance. It's still college athletics, so soccer takes up a lot of your time and life. But I absolutely loved it there."

It was in the fall of 2016 that Kaepernick knelt. Maya said, "I was just really thinking about what a powerful move that was for him to do, and what a risk he took, by being a Black man and taking a knee during the anthem on a national stage. I was also mortified by how people treated him and was trying to think about what is my role in this? I was thinking about whether I could do anything, or even if I should do anything. Then Megan Rapinoe knelt, and that set an example of using your privilege and saying, 'Yes, I'm a white woman, but I believe in Kaepernick and what he stands for, and I'm behind him.'"

Throughout the entire season, Maya thought about the pos-sibility of taking a knee: "How should I do it? What's the right way to do it? I was talking to my parents about it too, because we had a few really strong military families on the team. I knew that if I were going to do it, it mattered to me that I talk to my teammates about why, what it meant, and to see if anyone would join me."

Maya organized a team meeting to talk about what Kaepernick kneeling signified. "It was a much more difficult conversation than I anticipated. At Smith College, we're kind of in this beautiful 'social justice bubble,' but the soccer team definitely pulled some of the people who were from the military or more conservative backgrounds, so we had a very long, hashed-out conversation where people were getting really emotional about their experiences. I think we had maybe two girls from marginalized backgrounds on the team, and I was the only person from a city, so we had just a few voices in the room talking about witnessing police oppression. One girl talked about what it feels like to worry about your family. And then the students who had military parents were just angry that we would, in their minds, attack them by stepping on their anthem. We were just trying to take apart their argument and ask the question, 'How can that be an assault on you, when it's trying to call attention to an assault on a whole group of Americans?'"

Ultimately, the team decided that it would be left to the personal choice of the player. It was "terrifying," Maya remembered, as only one teammate ended up joining her. The response was "a huge mix." She recalled that "a lot of the parents were supportive. My parents were so proud they posted it on their Facebook. My dad is from a poor rural community in Ohio, and one of his high school classmates unfortunately took the picture—after being really angry and violent in his comments—and posted it on some kind of right-wing page, and then people were chiming in with really misogynistic and violent comments on my dad's picture. He eventually unfriended the person who posted the photo on that right-wing page. I know he got very angry at how horrible people were."

This made Maya reflect on how being a woman affected the social media backlash that she encountered. "I know when Rapinoe kneeled, she said she was kneeling to oppose police brutality against Black Americans, but part of her thing was being a woman, so there's a gender component as well, and how the flag doesn't represent everybody equally. I know her main motivation was police brutality against African Americans, but I didn't really wrap my head around whether gender would factor into my kneeling. But the comments and the backlash definitely took a misogynistic spin."

In speaking to her teammates who were connected to the military, "part of me wanted to point out this huge issue of militarization of sport and militarization of what it means to be a citizen. Also, if you're defending the country, apart from what everybody thinks America stands for is the ability to speak freely, speak your mind, and stand up for issues that matter to you and to engage in public discourse. That's why we have this Constitution and this First Amendment and everything everyone adamantly says that they fight for. But then if someone publicly and peacefully protests, if it has anything to do with the anthem, suddenly there's this huge backlash, even though they're doing what people are fighting for, right?"

When Maya heard that an NFL quarterback was taking a knee during the anthem, "I was excited. I knew that there'd be negative backlash, but I was ecstatic that someone was using such a powerful platform to call attention to an issue that most people weren't paying attention to. If the NFL is going to be this huge thing that represents America, then I was just really proud of him for using that. We've seen a few NFL players use their fame and celebrity, but to kneel during the anthem on live television must have been terrifying, especially as a Black man. It's a lot less risky for me, a white girl on a college field, to do it, of course. I hoped that it would start a national discourse to bring attention to issues that were being ignored. Think about his protest. It wasn't violent. It wasn't disrespectful. He was just making a public statement. There's just something about Blackness that makes certain people enraged. What times we are living in. How is it a peaceful protest bringing your gun to the Capitol building steps and threatening elected officials, and kneeling for the anthem isn't?"

As for any lessons she learned, "I was glad to able to use my privilege, in some way, to bring attention to an issue. As scary as it was, it was definitely worth it. It's not like the issue has gone away at all. In fact, it's getting worse. The more we can talk about it and fight this complacency, then maybe we can take some actual steps, once people open their eyes."

3

The Pros

True to form for someone from my generation, everything reminds me of The Simpsons, *and a central theme to* The Kaepernick Effect *is no exception. There is a scene in one episode where Homer refuses to believe Lisa that bacon, ham, and pork chops all come from the same animal. "Oh, sure, Lisa, a MAGIC animal!" Homer smirks. This is similar to how I feel about these high school, college, and professional athletes who protested during the anthem: they spring from the same source, but at the same time they are all very different. The professional protesting athlete certainly has a separate set of challenges from younger cohorts. The risks are different. The stakes are different. The punishments are different as well.*

These are the top 1 percent of athletes throughout the world. They are the ones who clawed their way through the competition of the Amateur Athletic Union, high school, and college athletics and found treasure on the other side. These are the people who have reached that brass ring and are actually getting paid—sometimes millions of dollars—for playing a game. These are people who were disproportionately born into economically disadvantaged backgrounds and have hit pay dirt. That often makes them responsible not only for their own financial fortunes but also for family and friends back home. When you also factor in that a typical pro career lasts only a few short years, this puts a tremendous amount of financial and personal pressure on pro athletes to toe the line and just shut up and play. But these constraints are also what gives political athletes their power. They are risking something by speaking out, and that makes people sit up and listen.

In a society defined by the silencing of the oppressed, pro sports is one of the few spaces where people who are poor and Black are given a platform and a microphone. That is why, as far back as the first Black heavyweight champion, Jack Johnson, more than a century ago, we have seen this platform policed so heavily by the powers that be in both ownership and the sports media. This is why Fox News told LeBron James to "shut up and dribble." It's not "politics" that they don't want in the sports world. It's a certain kind of politics. It's resistance politics. It's antiracist politics. The platform athletes enjoy must be used either to sell products or to mimic the politics of the bosses, or a price will be paid. Donald Trump in particular called for athletes to lose their jobs for daring to have antiracist political opinions—all while he appeared at political rallies with right-wing athletes. The rules of the game are clear.

This fresh age of resistance politics recalls the time when Muhammad Ali had his title stripped away following his resistance to the Vietnam War draft. Then, former champion Floyd Patterson wrote in Esquire, "The prizefighter in America is not supposed to shoot off his mouth about politics, particularly when his views oppose the Government's and might influence many among the

*working classes who follow boxing. . . . The prizefighter is consid-
ered by most people to be merely a tough, insensitive man, a dumb
half-naked entertainer wearing a muzzled mouthpiece."*

*In 2016, Colin Kaepernick refused to be muzzled. His actions
have had a catalytic effect on all athletes—but particularly pro
athletes—who have started to feel their own power. The athletic
industrial complex, including its allies in the media, immediately
went into motion to ensure that Kaepernick would become a cau-
tionary tale. They exiled him from the league after a top-notch
season on an inept team. But that didn't stop a layer of pro athletes from attempting to "stand with Kap" and prevent him from
being isolated.*

*The athletes who kept the struggle alive at the professional
level from 2016 to 2020 accomplished an incredibly important
task. They did not let Kaepernick become the ghost story. Because
they did so, an entire generation of young athletes have come of
age in the past five years who see Kaepernick as someone to emu-
late, not someone whose story provokes fear.*

In the iconic photos of Colin Kaepernick taking a knee, you
will always see Eric Reid kneeling right next to him. Eric is
an NFL safety who has been Kaepernick's most effective advocate inside and outside the league. In addition, Reid has been
a part of the Know Your Rights Camps that Kaepernick has put
on in cities around the country, educating young people about
politics, nutrition, and their rights when confronted by law
enforcement.

Eric grew up in rural Louisiana. "For the most part, my parents did a good job of sheltering us from the issues of the world
like racism and police brutality, but being Black in America,

eventually I experienced some of it. I remember driving to get my hair cut when I was in high school. I just got my driver's license, so I was driving alone. And on the way, I saw a burning cross in broad daylight in somebody's yard. It was obviously really bizarre, and I couldn't really believe what I was seeing, couldn't really believe that this was really happening right now."

As for encounters with police, "I think there was always some level of discomfort when you encounter a police officer— at least that's always been my reality," he said. "It didn't occur to me why that was until I was in college, when I got the understanding that it's because it was meant to be that way. The officer intended for it to be that way. There was an occurrence in college while I was staying out with a cousin. We were at a Mellow Mushroom. If you're not familiar with Mellow Mushroom, it's a pizza place that turns into a kind of nighttime hangout spot where they play music. It starts to get to closing time and police were there, starting to tell people to go home. Well, like college kids do, everybody just kind of stood around and kept their conversation going, even though the music had stopped. And I mean, everybody there was still there. Nobody had really left yet. Then this officer walks up and grabs my cousin, who just so happened to be talking to a white girl who was our friend. He grabs my cousin by the collar and yanks him and says, 'I said it's time to go home.' And I'm like, 'Yo! There are so many people in here right now! Why did you just walk up on my cousin and grab him?' There's no other reason in my mind that makes sense other than the fact that my Black cousin was talking to a white female. I very ignorantly approached the officer and said, 'What is going on? Why are you holding my cousin like this?' He proceeds to tell me that my cousin was, basically, being belligerent with him. I say, 'I just watched this entire thing unfold. You came up out of nowhere.' He then says back, 'I wouldn't be a jerk to the guy with a gun.' So there it was. He said that word, "gun," in that moment, threatening us with his authority to pull his gun on us. That was my real first occurrence. Like, wow: my cousin was talking to a white girl and the police officer could've cost us our lives."

On the 49ers, Reid's step toward activism grew out of his faith. "I had just finished reading the Bible and I was trying to get clarity in my walk with faith, and I just became really distraught with what was happening in the world," he said. "I felt like because I had the platform, I should use that to do some sort of good, so that whenever I looked back on my career, I could say that I tried. But really the police killing of Alton Sterling comes to mind because he was killed in Baton Rouge, Louisiana, which was fifteen minutes from where I grew up. I was actually born in Baton Rouge. My dad worked at LSU. I had family members in Baton Rouge. It could have been anybody that I knew or loved. That really drove me to wanting to do something."

Eric is at peace with the backlash his stance has provoked. "I can honestly say the threats that I saw were all internet warriors: people that felt very comfortable typing something on social media. I can't recall a single time somebody had that same tone or demeanor in an in-person encounter. I had people say that they disagree with me in person. I'm not saying that didn't happen, but it's never been in a threatening type of environment."

As of this writing, Reid is an unsigned free agent, despite being ranked as one of the best safeties in the game. It is difficult to believe that his politics don't have something to do with it. But he is fortified by his faith in the face of all doubters. "I believe that what I was doing was for the Lord. For me, what it boils down to was: Am I the man that I believe that I am? Am I really following Christ in how I live my life? You can lie to other people, but can you lie to yourself? Am I a hypocrite in my own space? I really just wanted to do something that I thought was going to be pleasing to the Lord, and I hope that it was."

I asked Eric what his reaction was when he heard about all these young people, particularly the high schoolers, picking up the torch and taking a knee. He said, "I was in awe of their courage to do what we were doing as adults as children. Because I know what we were dealing with and I know in a lot of ways the environment that kids are in, being in school, that social setting can be tougher than the social setting that adults experience. We all remember how tough it was being kids in school, trying to be the cool kid, trying to not be bullied or just trying to navigate that weird time in your life. For the kids that wanted to stand up for folks, I just think it took a lot of mental fortitude."

His message for them is that "love is the key. Don't become so consumed in this fight that you lose your love for people, because the reason I started doing this, the reason Colin started doing this, was out of our love for folks who were murdered. Just as Christ loved us so much that he gave his life for our sins, we are called to love people. Don't let what they've done to us become hatred."

I asked Reid, as a close friend of Kaepernick, if the Colin he knew in 2016 was the same Colin he knows today. He said,

"I think Colin has grown. Is he done growing? I hope not. Am I done growing? I hope not. Are you done growing? I hope not. I think we're all continuing to grow and learn. That doesn't mean that everything we've done in the past has been right, or righteous, or correct, but the intent that we all should have is to do things in love. If you do things in love, it's hard to be malicious."

As for the NFL and its efforts to now look more engaged on racial justice issues, Reid said, "I think the NFL cares about its bottom line. Are there good people in the NFL? Sure there are. I think people in the NFL care about certain aspects of what is going on in the world, but I think their key concern is their bottom line. You can look at the history of all the decisions they've made. You can look at what's happening currently in the CBA [the NFL's collective bargaining agreement] and the massive reduction in benefits to disabled players that were promised to them for life. It's hard to say that you care about somebody when you're changing something that you said they could have for the rest of their life. But remember that we need to do this because we love one another. Don't let the evilness that's happened to us or somebody you know manifest itself as hatred in your heart. Do this because you love each other, because that's the only way you'll have peace."

Bruce Maxwell was a catcher for the Oakland A's until he was cast out of the league for kneeling during the national anthem. His blackballing has garnered considerably less coverage than that of Kaepernick. (Maxwell was eventually offered a minor league contract by the Mets in July 2020.)

Maxwell grew up in Huntsville, Alabama, raised by his Black

father and white mother. "It was interesting," he said. When he was ten years old, Bruce played in a baseball tournament in Cullman, Alabama, home to the founder of Alabama's KKK. "We beat the home team for the championship, and as we're getting our awards and whatnot, someone from Cullman came out and told us to get home before they hang us."

Another time the team was driving on a highway at midnight in Pulaski, Tennessee, and all of a sudden, "I look up and I see a group of men in white sheets walking into the woods, off of the highway. Torches, tiki torches—I mean, you name it, they had it. I looked at my dad and he said, 'Yes, it is what you think it is, and no, we're not going to talk about it.'"

When Bruce was growing up, his father was "ex-military, he dressed well, and even with all that, had to deal with racial profiling." That seared itself into Bruce's young mind. So did the fact that "my mother got called a n——er-lover when we were growing up because she's married to and has kids with a Black man."

Bruce came to kneeling because he was trying to figure out how to make a difference in a sport with a paucity of Black Americans. "Baseball's always been my life. I love pro ball. We represent so many countries and so many ethnicities around the world. It's amazing. I have a lot of good friends that are Latino. I have a lot of good friends that are Asian, and what we share is a love of the game. But once Kaepernick started kneeling, I was sitting there, studying what he was doing and thinking, 'How can I do this?' We were in season, and Donald Trump had a rally in Alabama. It was even in Huntsville, in our civic center. That was the moment he called the NFL players that were kneeling 'sons of bitches' and that they should be out on the street. That really pushed me all the way over the edge. To see people where I'm from support that and the people where I'm from support that our president is calling people out by their name because of the color of their skin and not because they've done anything wrong. That was too much. Just to see that support of the bigotry, the racism, and the bullshit that he was feeding America."

Maxwell was attracted to a kneeling protest before a game because "I'm a firm believer in our right to free speech and protest. These guys weren't disruptive, by any means. The disruptors are ones who just want us to shut up and play our sport. People always say don't bring politics into sports. Sports are political. You can't tell me that every person on every team is there just because of their performance. Also, you have to do appearances. You have to do activities in the community. All of those are political things. Now Black players, especially the ones at the top of your athletic threshold, are taking notice and now they're wanting to speak up and take stands."

Before Maxwell took the knee that would exile him from the major leagues, he called his father and his aunt, both ex-military, both of whom told him that they supported him 100 percent. Then he held a meeting with A's manager Bob Melvin and the team general manager, David Forst. "I said to them, 'Listen, shit that's going on right now, it's not fair. I'm not okay with it. It's bothering me. So this is what I want to do. This is why I'm going to do it. This is some of the shit that I've gone through with my family, including my sister, my dad, and my mom. I'm doing this for my people. I know you don't understand. You want to understand but you can't, because of the color of your skin. You don't choose to be born white. I don't choose to be born biracial. It is what it is, but this is what I want to do. If you guys have any objections to the fact that maybe this takes away from the spotlight on the team in a positive way, or if you are concerned that it could cause harm to you or your families or to my teammates, you stand up now and you tell me and I won't do it and I'll find another way. But for me, this is the way I want to get my point across and get this stance heard in the greatest magnitude possible.'"

Bruce said they both supported him without reservation. He recalled that they said, "You're going to get shit. Shit's going to come our way, but we support your personal beliefs and what you believe in."

Then Bruce did the same thing with all twenty-five of his teammates in the locker room. "I had our trainers. I had our strength coaches. I had our batboys, every one of them. I stood up in the middle of our lockers in Oakland, and I explained to them what was going to happen, what I wanted to do, and why. I stood up and I told them, 'This shit has been eating at me forever. The rally Trump just had was in my hometown. To see the people that I know and see the families that I know, that I grew up around, support this asshole and degrade my people for the color of their skin just because they want a change because we're getting treated unequally in our own supposedly free country. . . . I can't sit there and stand anymore. If any of you guys, any of you, any coaches, staff, batboys, anything, if any of you fear for your career or fear that you're going to get labeled that you're a teammate of mine, or you fear that you're going to get messages of being a n——er-lover or anything like that, from fans to your family, stand up right now and tell me that you don't want me to do it, and I won't do it. I didn't come in here to cause problems. I don't want to distract you guys from playing baseball. My job here is not to tell you to defend me. I can defend myself. I'm a grown-ass man. This is my personal choice.'"

Not one person stood up and objected. Not one coach member, not one staff member, not one batboy. "I felt like I went about it the right way. I had the utmost support, supposedly, from the whole staff, from my teammates. Everybody knew. Everybody was aware."

After he took a knee in this most conservative of sports, the threats rolled in fast and furious, and they weren't just directed at Bruce. "There was an incident where I had a guy who had sent my sister messages and found out where my mom lived. He told me that he would go and blow up my sister's school and her gym where she coached in Texas. I had to call the sheriff of her town and put a detail on my sister for two weeks. To find out that a dude took the time to find out where my mother lived, I called her and I said, 'This is the shit that's going on.'

"I talked to my stepdad at the time. I told the media, 'You want to go after my dad? Good luck. He's a crazy-ass dude. He's ex-military. He's paranoid as hell. You go ahead and try to go after him. I'll even give you his fucking home address. That's fine by me. But if you go after the women in my life, I promise you'll see a different me.' I told them, it's one thing fucking typing on the internet; it's another thing to be about it. I said to a friend, 'I will leave here and go to my family's aid in a heartbeat and accept the consequences that come after that. Nobody, as long as I'm breathing, will harm my family. Especially the women in my family.'"

But Bruce said that despite what he and his family went

through, he would do it again. "The fact of the matter is that the purpose is greater than me putting my cleats on every day in the big leagues. I loved my time out there, but what came after was the direct aftermath of what had happened."

Three years later and playing in Mexico, Bruce still deals with the consequences of his decision. "I had a guy reach out to me in the middle of my season, last year, to tell me he hoped I burned in a house fire. If I didn't die, he said he wanted me to live with severe, third-degree burns for the rest of my life. Verbatim, that was the message. I've really distanced myself, especially last year, so I could focus on what I was doing down here, and I still had people find me, just to send me nasty shit."

I asked Bruce why he was the only person to do this in baseball and why no one publicly supported him when he found himself out of work that off-season, with no contract offers on the table. "It's because of the lack of color—the lack of Black Americans—in baseball. One hundred percent. That's why when I was asked if I expected anybody to follow suit and also take a knee, I said, 'No, I know how this game works. We've got guys in the league that are worried about money, security for their family.' I understand that. But what I don't understand is why some of the older guys in the league who were some of my mentors, some of my big brothers, didn't say anything. Adam Jones has been speaking out about it for years. He told me, 'Honestly, kid, I wish it didn't have to be you. It should've been a veteran, someone who had status in the game. But you handled it right, and I'm right here if you need me.' He came out and spoke about it. I understand why other guys did not say shit. But at the same time, I put that cause over my career. I had a lot to lose personally. I only had a year in the league. I wasn't rich by any means. But I was like, 'Fuck it. I don't have kids. I don't have anyone that's dependent on me, but this right here is something that I need to do, because this shit's eating me up inside.' The game of baseball is just different than the NFL or NBA because in these sports, your top players are African Americans. These are the players making the most money, selling the most jerseys and the most tickets."

It's not just about the lack of Black American stars. According to Maxwell, it's also rooted in the ways that baseball is both a very individualized and a very team-oriented sport. "I've played with a lot of people who are team-first. I've played with a whole helluva lot of people who are me-first, because it's about making money. It really is. But at the end of the day, that shows me who my true friends are when it comes to the game of baseball in the States. I know who's confident about themselves and where they come from. It shows me a lot about people. So I don't talk to a lot of people that I used to since I've been out of MLB, and I'm totally okay with that."

The reality is that Bruce Maxwell was blackballed. "It feels like shit, personally. It's a battle I go through every day. When you get judged and denied an opportunity due to a personal belief . . . this is what I live with. Baseball and MLB say they're all about putting your best nine on the field, regardless of what you look like or what you sound like, or whatever that bullshit is. At the end of the day, they want to preach about being all about who can deliver the best stats, but it is all lies. This last year, I was a leader for my team, and to not get any interest in the off-season, even from teams that really are in dire need of catching, because of the way baseball has labeled me over the last two years, that sucks. It feels like shit."

Sure enough, Bruce's record has been stellar in Mexico, but it still hasn't merited him any interest. "I came down here and we turned this pitching staff and their mind-sets around, to win the championship. First time ever in our team's history. To do what I did and to play as much as I did and to not even get any interest? That speaks volumes."

What Maxwell believes is that institutionalized racism is built into the game. It's not just politics or taking a knee. It's prejudice against Black American players. "It goes beyond production. It depends on who you are. If you're a high-profile guy and you are white, you get more lenient eyes on you. If you're Latin, if you're Black, you might not get the same leniency. You might have a harder road, you might have a harder time to get to the big leagues. I was a second-rounder dude."

Maxwell goes on to say that he sees this as a microcosm of U.S. society. "People always say to me, 'Oh, always bringing in the race card.' I shoot right back with, 'No, you say that I bring race cards, because you've never had to deal from that deck.' I know so many people that have ridiculous qualifications and ridiculous athletic ability that played baseball that couldn't get into the league."

Sentiments like this kept Maxwell out of baseball and he knows it. "You're LeBron James, you're Dwyane Wade, those dudes can't be touched. If LeBron James dropped out of the league because he's getting unfair treatment for race, shit, half the league's losing revenue and fans. It's just different in the game of baseball. They forget about you and can write you off and they get to because all of our owners are white." I asked Bruce about his union, the Major League Baseball Players Association. He said, "The Players Association didn't fucking help me. I was out there on my own. It took them three months to reach out to me and it's because I called [MLBPA president] Tony Clark. Nobody had reached out to me. There was no communication to defend my honor. There was nothing about talking about trying to get this shit worked out. I had nothing. I was literally trapped in my apartment."

I asked Bruce about the league celebrating Jackie Robinson every year. He said, "I think the game of baseball is super hypocritical. We have less than 1 percent African American coaches and 7 percent African American players in our sport, but they pride themselves on Jackie Robinson Day and they make the jerseys and make all these promotions and shit. They make so much money off of these promotions, and yet they don't give African Americans the same opportunities that they give whites in the game of baseball. They're quick to judge them negatively. They have them on a short leash. I've played with guys who've gotten numerous opportunities to fail and keep failing and still got promoted and an opportunity because they're white. It's hypocrisy at its finest. Jackie Robinson paved the way for us to be able to play in the MLB, but at the same time, I hate celebrating it, because it's bullshit. He means the world to us African American players. Even the Latin dudes. In white people's eyes, they're Black too. To have the barrier knocked down and the opportunity to play in the big leagues is great, but our road to the big leagues is still a lot harder and it's a lot longer, too, to get there, depending on what team you play for. I think it's hypocritical bullshit. They sit here and try to pride themselves, 'Thank you, Jackie, thank you, Jackie,' but they get rid of us all the time, dude."

Maxwell feels a personal affinity with Colin Kaepernick.

"Me and Kaepernick, we both wake up Black," he said. "We probably experience shit down the road a little differently than each other, but we're still Black. We still look Black. We are still of Black descent. He walks out of his house and he's Black, every single day. People try to discredit anybody who tries to buck the normalcy of our country, and the normalcy is white supremacy."

Gwen Berry is a record-setting competitor in the hammer throw and a three-time world champion. "When I was in high school, I used to do the triple jump and some running events. And when I was recruited to a school in Illinois, my coach said, 'You're kind of big. You won't lose any weight because you're just naturally big-boned. You could try something else. You could try something different.'"

When the hammer throw was suggested, Gwen said no. She answered in the negative because "I wasn't *that* big and I wasn't strong and I had never thrown in my life. I didn't even know what the hammer throw was. Well, I tried it and I almost made the Junior Olympic team in three months."

After winning the gold medal in the 2019 Pan American Games, she raised her fist on the medal stand. Another athlete at those games, the fencer Race Imboden, took a knee. The ensuing controversy provoked the Olympics to demand that no political expression take place during the games, but this has not stopped Gwen from continuing to be outspoken against censorship and for Black lives. She has chosen to go on a full campaign, expressed on social media and in the op-ed pages of the *New York Times*, to demand that her voice—and the voices of other Olympic athletes—be heard.

It's her very history that informs her relentlessness. Gwen went to high school in Ferguson, Missouri—the same Ferguson that saw Michael Brown killed by Darren Wilson in 2014. "It was a tough upbringing," she recalled. "My granny had like thirteen people in her house at one time, and we were all living together." The first time she had her own bedroom was in college. Growing up in Ferguson was "pretty tough. I remember my uncle used to tell me stories about how the police used to harass them. They used to have to fight or do this or that, and I really didn't understand it until I got older."

The police killing of Michael Brown in Ferguson was something that Gwen took really hard "because I literally grew up around the corner where he got shot. Like the same street. My house . . . you could've hopped the fence and then you'd be right where he was shot. I was in college at the time, so I flew back to St. Louis and just walked the streets, felt the tension and felt how hard the community took it. It was crazy. It was unreal, honestly. I couldn't believe it. I felt like I didn't know what the world meant to me. What living in America really meant. I couldn't understand why the cop in this situation didn't take the necessary precautions to make sure that at least Michael Brown lived. Or make better decisions to maybe stay in the car or call for backup. Anything. I felt like it could've been handled a different way. I just couldn't understand why that situation led to a kid's death."

The killing of Brown compelled Gwen to think about her own family, if they had been in Brown's situation. "I couldn't help asking myself: 'What if that killing had been meant for my uncle? What if it had been meant for my other friends? What could it have meant for me? What could it have meant for my child?' I just really didn't understand what America meant to me anymore."

Then she raised that fist on the medal stand. "My approach has always been to fight. Because growing up, we had to fight, we had to run, we had to do different things to survive. You see drug dealers, the crime, homeless people, crackheads, you see so many unfortunate things and it's a Black community. There's not a white person in sight. So I feel like there were things that resonated with me and it made me realize that when people are trying to make a change, they do it for a reason. They see the things that I see and they feel the way that I feel. Like, literally, there was probably a lot of death in Ferguson—young Black men getting killed in Ferguson—and I wouldn't have even known. I hadn't been aware of things that were going on. For me, the first thing was awareness. We have to bring awareness to what this system is doing to these Black mothers and these Black fathers. Because we do matter. Our kids have to see the truth even though they'll forever be traumatized by this. School is easy. College is easy. But when you get into the real world, you really see how your color and how you were raised affects everything that you do. Everything."

Gwen wasn't nervous before raising her fist, even knowing what the fallout would be. "I want to speak for those people who I see every day before practice, who I grew up with. I want to speak for those people because I don't agree with what's going on in this country, point-blank."

When Gwen's fist was in the air, the feeling was "peace. I felt like I finally did something that I wanted to do and was free to do. I struggled a lot in my athletic career and it was a tough meet. I felt like all Black children on that medal stand.

We always grow up in tough environments. It's always hard for us. I feel like that meet resonated with my life and the lives of other people that I know. When I raised my fist, I was like, 'I did it!' I was at peace. I was saluting everybody who's ever had a hard childhood or whoever thought that they couldn't make it. To show them, I stand with you. I'm here with you too. I've experienced that too."

The backlash experienced by Berry was ferocious. "Of course, the 'go back to Africa' line came through to me. I also received a lot of death threats. I lost sponsorships. I lost funding from grants. I had just recently made the Olympic team. I was doing it in an Olympic uniform with 'USA' across my chest. It wasn't too tough for me, but the only thing that hurt was my finances. I lost a lot by making a stand."

The United States Olympic & Paralympic Committee put Berry on probation for twelve months, meaning that over the next year, she couldn't repeat her actions from the Pan American Games: no fist raising, no taking a knee, no politics, no nothing. The USOPC put out a statement condemning her actions. Gwen said, "It's really a smack in the face because I've lost so much. . . . I didn't cause any altercations. There was nothing that I did that was wrong. All I did was speak out about who I stand with, what I stand for, and how I felt. My family has lost so much because of the reprimands. It's just hypocrisy. But I feel like that is America. They say a thousand things, but they do the opposite. That's the country we live in and that's why so many people are upset right now."

Despite that, Gwen has no regrets. "I feel like if you regret the things you do, then you really don't know why you're doing it. I know why I did it and I know who I helped and who I inspired. The first thing that people can hurt you with is the money, but that's material. Money's not my guide, so no regrets for me."

When Berry's thoughts turn to Kaepernick, her analysis turns to the question of power. "I feel like every other great Black person: he's being blackballed. It speaks, again, to this country. When certain people are in charge, they like to stay in charge. So what do they do? They protect their assets. They protect their income. The NFL has billions of dollars at stake. So if you're in charge, you don't want anyone messing up your billions of dollars. When somebody speaks out about things that are too hard to handle, the people in power are the reason why some of these things are happening so they're going to shut this dissent down! Kaepernick is one of the best quarterbacks that we've had in a while, but why shut him down if he's speaking on the truth? That's the irony of America. America is always like, 'Freedom of this, freedom of that. We fight for this. Unity,' and all of this stuff, but as soon as somebody challenges the core of America, or what we're supposed to stand for, it's a problem. That's irony. I don't understand that. They raise the flag, they sing the anthem, yet they're killing Black and Brown children everywhere for nothing. It's crazy. I feel like what he did was really bold. He was willing to take the sacrifice, which a lot of people, to this day, will not. They aren't willing to do it. They're not willing to do it because they're scared of the finances. That's the number one thing. If everyone had the same amount of money, or if everyone didn't have any money, more people would come and take a stand. But when you make a ton of money, you don't want to lose that, so you say, 'Nah, I'm not saying something. I stand with him, but in silence, though.'

"I can't tell people to take a stand. I can't tell people to
something that's controversial, or speak the truth, but I feel like
the more that people do, the more the money cannot control
athletes. I feel like our athletic abilities are not our only asset.
If you think about it, what's the point of being the greatest athlete in the world, if you can't do something with it? One of our
assets is our voice. We're idolized. We're highly sought after.
It shouldn't just be about what we can do on the court or in
the field of play. We have to give back to our communities. We
have to promote change or else our kids are going to grow up
in the same system we grew up in and it will do nothing for
them. I feel like that's what Kaepernick did. That's what I plan
to do. That's what a lot of athletes paved the way for us to do.
And they lost a lot, but they inspired masses of people along
the way."

I asked if she felt vindicated given the protests that were
sweeping the country over the summer of 2020. She said, "I
definitely think the demonstrations vindicate me. I feel like for
once in my life, I'm finally being understood. I know I spoke
out last year, and let's be honest, I got more hate than love. Like
I said, I lost a lot, and therefore my family lost a lot. At that
time, I felt misunderstood. I felt like my fellow competitors
were scared to come out and stand with me because athletes
lose so much, and they have families to feed. So right now, I
definitely feel vindicated. It helped me also to go out there and
support my people, and march with my people, and protest. I'm
pretty ecstatic right now. I just hope that everyone keeps the
momentum going. We have to come up with ideas, we have to
strategize, we have to plan, and momentum is everything."

• • •

eceiver for the Houston Texans, has never
nee during the national anthem at NFL
done more than that. Stills has taken his
turf to the streets, getting arrested at Black
ests in Louisville to bring justice in the case
of ᴅ.ᴵ.ᴵ., an EMT killed by three police officers who
received no punishment—not even an indictment—for the
killing.

Kenny grew up in Oceanside, California, which is right near
the military base Camp Pendleton. "My mom raised five kids.
I was the last of her five children. I started playing football at
a young age, six years old. From the time that I started playing
ball, all of my coaches were Marines. My mentor and the coach
that I had from age seven all the way until when I was in high
school at fifteen, he served in the Marines."

These coaches preached a Marine-style discipline. There
was no stepping out of line. "We went to the Pop Warner Super
Bowl in Orlando and played at the Disney sports complex," he
said. "While we were there, we walked around everyplace in
two lines. We didn't make a sound. They wrote a letter to our
staff after we left there—we were the most well-behaved team
they had ever seen come through there."

For Kenny, this life of hyperdisciplined football took place in
an environment that was predominantly Black. "It wasn't until
I got to college, moving to Oklahoma, going to Dallas. . . . That
was the first time I had people look at me differently, look at
my friends differently, because of the color of our skin. We had
an encounter with a police officer, where we were with a friend
who was a future Oklahoma student as well. She was showing

us around Dallas and we went to a game. She was intoxicated, so we were trying to help take care of her, take her home, this young woman with three Black guys. We're in public trying to carry her back to the car and get her situated and help find her friends. The police then come up to us, and they say, 'Hey, you know it's illegal to solicit sex in the state of Texas?' or some shit. We were like, 'What?' We didn't even understand what he was saying, because he thought that we were pimping out this girl. He thought we were pimps. Then another situation happened later that same evening, again when we were harassed by police. That was the first time that I really felt like, wow, this is something you see in the movies or something that you thought would have happened back in the day, something that was in our past: being extremely intimidated and scared of the police, thinking that I might not even go home tonight."

Kenny was never politically active growing up. But it was the experience of seeing police murders on camera, coupled with the 2016 elections, that compelled him to act. He first took a knee before an NFL game on September 11, 2016. "I knew the repercussions that were going to come from it," he said. "Especially it being September 11, especially knowing the men and women that have helped raise me. I'm talking every sport that I played. If the coach wasn't in the military, their dad was. Just understanding that and understanding that I was in a contract year, knowing that it could affect my future and my family's future. The fear I felt was real. I can remember my heart racing a million miles per hour. Just being scared, intimidated, nervous of what could come next. I called my coach the night before the game, and I told him that I was thinking about getting involved in the protest, and he basically asked me if I wouldn't get involved. I told him, 'Thank you for your opinion, but I'm going to sleep on it and pray on it and kind of go from there.'"

When Kenny woke up in the morning, "in my heart and in my gut, I felt like it was the right thing to do. I felt like if I didn't act or didn't get involved, then I'd be missing out on my opportunity to use my voice, to use my platform. It took me feeling like enough is enough with this stuff I'm seeing on TV and on social media. I got to a point where I was feeling genuinely hopeless. What happens if this happens to me or my family members or anyone? What are we going to do? How do we do something about this?"

Kenny had seen Kaepernick, Eric Reid, and Megan Rapinoe taking a knee and thought, "This is my way of getting involved. This is how I can say that this isn't okay. This is my way of letting these families know that we're with them and we see them and we're going to do something about this. I didn't want to miss out on my opportunity to use my voice."

What makes Kenny Stills special is that, like Eric Reid, he kept taking a knee long after Kaepernick had been exiled from the league and long after it had ceased to become something that even a minority of players were doing. He kept the flame lit "because overall, there hasn't been any progress. There are cases that continue to happen where the system plays in favor of law enforcement. I want to continue to let families know that there are groups of people out there that see that and that we're with them. I think it's an act of solidarity, one. And two, it's also a genuine feeling of how I feel. I don't feel represented by that song, or that flag, or the things that we say that we're about, but we're not actually fulfilling."

As for Kaepernick, Kenny only was aware of him as "a damn good football player" before 2016. "He was a baller. That's really all I knew. I remember watching him in college play at Nevada. It was a Saturday night game and he just took over. That left an imprint on my mind. Watching him develop, grow, and make it to a Super Bowl and all the things that he's done, I just was like, 'Damn, this dude's a baller!' But now I've spent a lot more time with him. I know that he cares about his people and that he wants to play ball. He's somebody that understands and knows what he's doing. You know, he's very calculated in the moves that he makes. He just wants to do what is right for his people and he wants to play ball and represent his people in that way, too."

I asked Kenny Stills what he'd say to the young athletes taking a knee in obscurity, in order to start conversations or spur activism in their communities. "I'd tell them to continue to educate themselves on our histories and on the system of government that's in place and the people that have been involved in this type of work before them. There's so much that we can learn from our history. The more that we can educate ourselves and be able to deliver the information clearly, I think people will start to understand and see for themselves that this protest, it's not for no reason. It's justified. There's a lot of work to do and we've got to continue to put our brains together to try and make a change and make a difference so that the next generation, their kids, don't have to come up in the same situation."

One way that Kenny has changed is that, he said, "I've shifted to just more human rights, overall, because I understand and see how we are all in this thing together. That means any group that's been marginalized. We're all in this thing together and we're all stronger together. That's my focus. As soon as I took a knee, I went straight to the local police officers and went to their check-in sessions before they go out to work. I'd go and stand up in front of them and say, 'Hey, my name's Kenny Stills, I was one of the players taking a knee and I'm here to tell you that we are not against police officers. We are against bad police officers. If you're going to be mad at me or upset with me because I don't like bad policing? Then we can't be on the same page. We just want good police officers in our neighborhoods. If you do something wrong, or make a mistake, well, that's un-derstandable. That happens. But for there to be no justice to be served, for there to be no apologies, for there to be nothing to come from a situation, and just act like nothing ever happened? That's not okay. From human to human, that's not okay.'"

Leah Tysse took a knee while singing the national anthem for the NBA's Sacramento Kings. Leah is an independent re-cording artist in the Bay Area. "My music, I would say, is soul-singer-songwriter-based music with funk, blues, and R & B as the base of it. As a freelancer, those are sort of genres that I work in. Also, gospel and Latin jazz. You've got to keep it versa-tile to make a living in this business as a freelancer."

Leah had been scheduled to sing the anthem at that game for several months. "I'm not sure exactly when I booked it. It was before Colin Kaepernick was starting to take a knee," she said. "So I didn't take the gig with the intention of mak-ing it a protest. Once things started to escalate, we started to learn more about the extended lyrics of the anthem and also that things were—and continue to be—out of control with po-lice. There was Oscar Grant in 2009, Trayvon Martin in 2012, and then around that time, 2014, 2015, 2016, there was Eric Garner, Michael Brown, Sandra Bland, Walter Scott, Tamir Rice, Philando Castile, Freddie Gray, Alton Sterling, Terence Crutcher—all these people of color were being executed by police for no reason. A traffic stop, a lot of traffic stops, also just being profiled, and it isn't happening to white people. It reached a boiling point. We're going through it again, and it never really stops. I think when there's video, then it becomes something that ends up on the news, people can see it. It's happening all the time and it's not a surprise to a lot of people. It doesn't ever stop."

Leah said that she felt like she had a choice in front of her. "I could sing the national anthem and just do nothing. I could not sing the anthem and just tell them I'm not going to do it. Or I can use my voice for something—in this case, an act of solidarity and protest, and I felt it was my duty and I had been placed in that position for a reason. I wanted to be an ally."

Leah wasn't scared but did feel some jitters. "I was in Sacramento and I live in the Bay Area, so in the Bay Area, it's a different climate than Sacramento. I'm not super familiar with Sacramento other than it's a little more conservative than it is [in the Bay Area], so I didn't know how they would react, how the actual crowd in the arena would react."

As she was leaving the court, people were supportive: no boos, nothing thrown in her direction. "I don't know what the people there were thinking, exactly. I know there were some people that I could see they knew what I was doing and they were supporting it. And then maybe others just didn't get it, I don't know. But it wasn't the immediate negative reaction in the arena that I expected."

Leah said, "You're taking a risk, sometimes, to do that, but at the end of the day, I think you have to do what's right. That's all we've got. I was hoping to help some people that maybe haven't thought about this issue—police brutality, white privilege, the environment of hatred and systemic racism that a lot of people who look like me don't experience. I'm white and a lot of people like me can't even really see it. They may see things on the news and see different videos, but they could still live their lives without really having to think about it. I was hoping to touch some people who hadn't really thought about it and just bring awareness. Because if I'm willing to use my voice, maybe somebody who hadn't really thought about it will do so and this could change their life and change their community, and maybe change even more."

Megan Rapinoe, her hair a shock of pink, dominated the sports world in 2019. She was the best player on the U.S. Women's National Team that brought home the World Cup. She was an outspoken advocate for social justice and she was the best interview in sports. Call it the Ali Trifecta.

Rapinoe first became truly known beyond the soccer world when she took a knee in 2016 in solidarity with Colin Kaepernick. When I spoke with her in 2020, amid the national demonstrations following the police murder of George Floyd, she said to me, "Everything is on fire and rightfully so."

Megan grew up in the small city of Redding, California, but it was the wider world that taught her about the depths of racism in America. She said, "I always think of racism in two ways. There is interpersonal racism—are you a racist; do you say the N-word—and then there's the systematic racial injustice that's rooted in how our country was founded, what we can call systematic oppression. I didn't learn about that history until my midtwenties maybe, and then I dove in with my support of Colin. But growing up, I knew you weren't supposed to say the N-word to Black people. I knew that there was racism. I knew about Nazism and swastikas, white power, and all that kind of stuff. I saw *American History X* with Ed Norton. That was my education. But I also knew about this in a kind of far-off way, like, 'Yeah, you shouldn't be racist.' But what does that even mean? And it's way more complicated than that. I think my process of going to college, leaving religion behind, starting to think on my own, and coming out as gay was all formative. I was like, 'Oh, I'm being judged for something I have no control over.' I wanted to support gay marriage and become more vocal, and that meant needing to understand oppression systemically. I'm asking people to be allies and asking for people to support me, even though they're not gay. I'm in the middle of wage battles with the federation, going through different collective bargaining agreements, realizing that, oh, we're probably not being treated fairly. All of that."

Megan's experience and sensitivities were heightened by the fact that her brother was in the criminal justice system and dealt with drug abuse. She saw firsthand how this country harms human beings through the never-ending "war on drugs."

Then the Ferguson uprising took place in 2014. By 2016, Megan said to herself, "I get it." She said that growing up, "you can look back on the civil rights movement and you can see the beatings, the fire hoses, and the dogs, and all of that. You can say, 'Wow, of course the South was racist at that time. Of course the police were racist and an extension of Jim Crow, which is an extension of slave catchers,' and all of that. I think I finally realized that there are Jim Crow practices that persist to this day. As Ferguson was happening, I was learning about the Black Lives Matter movement. I learned more in 2015, and then by 2016, that was when everything was more clear to me and I was ready to act."

Everything changed when Megan took a knee during the anthem. "I don't think I was debating it in my mind that much. That summer was wild, horrific. We get past the Olympics, we come home. Very quickly Colin starts kneeling. I was listening to everything that he was saying and everything that everyone else was saying in response. Very quickly it was clear that nobody in power was wanting to hear what Colin trying to say. That's why they were saying all this stuff, conflating patriotism, military, and the flag. I was thinking that we all have a part to play. I was feeling like I've stood up for my own rights, but I've also asked people to stand up for my rights. It was my turn. It's also, like, duh, this is very clearly happening. This seems like a good form of protest. It's peaceful. We're being respectful. All these things. In the days leading up—actually [Megan's partner, WNBA star] Sue [Bird] didn't tell me this story until recently—I think it was two days before I knelt, I went to her game in Chicago. This was before we had started dating. Both our teams just happened to be playing there. I stayed seated during the national anthem and she saw it and didn't even tell me until a few months ago. So that was the first one, and then at my own game, I was like—of course, however many people I was going to be in front of. Not that many because the NWSL

[National Women's Soccer League] crowds aren't that big, but I knew it was time for me to do it. It wasn't a long, arduous decision. It was more like, 'Of course, this is something that I can do to help,' and maybe I was hoping that this was going to be sweeping. It is clear that it's happening. Tons of athletes are going to do it. Just do it, get on board, and help more people get comfortable doing it."

Megan was prepared to take the knee. The backlash was something else. "I don't know if I could've known what was coming. I mean, on the one hand, I was totally unprepared, because I didn't have a grand, master plan and didn't talk with anyone about it. The decision just kind of came and it seemed fine to me. I was ready to talk about it and I felt like I was able to talk about it in an intelligent way. I was able to bring it back to what we were actually talking about. I was able to defend Colin and defend myself. I felt good in that sense. But the fallout was wild! You have no idea! You never are really prepared for that, but that was all part of it. This is the work that needs to be done. My sister and I had a business together and that tanked and crashed. I wasn't dropped by any sponsors, but certainly wasn't getting any more. I didn't play for the national team for a long time. Obviously, the National Team Federation put out a statement that was ridiculous and missed the entire point, and still to this day is horrible. It made them look terrible. I don't know if I could've really been prepared for that, but I felt 100 percent solid in my action and I was ready to talk about it. I felt prepared in that way."

In Megan's mind, the gesture of taking a knee has taken on a greater resonance with time. "I think seeing Colin go through what he went through and the hate and vitriol, and changing of

the topic, and a lack of support from white people, white institutions, the government, the president, his own commissioner,
the owners in his league, it was very clear who was against it
and why. So I did sort of understand and feel in that moment,
'This is the symbol, okay.' You're peacefully kneeling, you're facing the flag, you're not turning your back. You're acting in a very
vulnerable position. From that perspective, this is probably the
symbol, like the fist had been at certain times in the past. In a
way, yes, you never know what the spark is going to be for the
revolution."

This also clarified for Megan the role of white people in
the struggle. "I think it's huge," she said. "It has to be huge.
It's a conscious choice, which makes it all the more damning
when you choose not to do it. For Black people, obviously, you
don't get to choose whether your skin is Black. You don't get to
choose when police roll up in your neighborhood and brutalize
you. You don't get to choose these things. For us, we do, and we
get to choose whether we want to put our skin in the game and
how much of it we want to put in the game. I think the role of
white people is huge. It also requires, I think, a commitment
to sacrificing the most and asking nothing in return. Do everything you can and at the end of the day stand behind everyone else. That's what it requires. We've been standing in front
and on top of everybody for-fucking-ever! So just take a step
back. It also requires a correction of your own people. That's
one of the hardest things: somebody kind of says something off-
hand and you could easily let it go, but you probably shouldn't.
So it requires the work in our own communities and with our
own families and our own friends to set an antiracist standard.
A slogan that's been going around the demonstrations is that

'silence is complicity,' and it absolutely is. Don't be an ally. Be an accomplice. If somebody's getting arrested, you should get arrested too. That's your gauge. If somebody's getting beat up, you should be right there getting beat up, too. I think that our role in this is tremendous because we benefit so much and we have benefited so much, and there's yet to be a true national reckoning and acknowledgment of and admission to what we did in the past and what we continue to do. Until we have that—and I don't think we get that without white people being very involved and committing to that—we're going to have this unrest."

Since this is a book centering on the young people—football players, volleyball players, soccer players, cheerleaders who at fifteen, sixteen, seventeen years old took a knee during the anthem and never got much publicity—I asked Megan if she had a message for those young people who, in anonymous fashion, took a knee and tried to start conversations over the last few years.

"I mean, incredibly courageous and, hey, follow the kids. I think Steve Kerr just said it: 'Follow the kids.' I think in a way, because they haven't lived full lives, have jobs, their identities aren't quite set, they have this sort of brazen approach of 'I'm going to do the right thing.' That sort of innocence and purity of it is just super inspiring. Just keep doing it, keep demanding it. That's the thing. We have the people. We have the support. We have the numbers. We just have to do it. We have to vote, we have to demand better, we have to protest, we have to walk, we have to kneel. We have to do all of these things. We have to demand it at a fever pitch."

Finally, I wanted to hear Megan's thoughts about the killing of George Floyd, the protests, and how they connect with what she was doing in 2016. "I feel like what we were doing and what Colin said in 2016 and why he said he was doing it, it's the same reason now. It's a system of oppression. It's an extension of slavery. It's meant to control people of color, to keep them down, and to not allow them life, liberty, and the pursuit of happiness. People are shockingly talking about the looting and the violence. I'm like, 'Oh, you don't like this kind of protest? You didn't like Colin's kind of protest. You didn't like when someone sat at a lunch-counter protest. You didn't like a fist up at the Olympics. You didn't like Muhammad Ali to talk about it. You didn't like Martin Luther King. You didn't like Malcolm X. You didn't like anybody, anything, anytime, ever, anywhere, that had to do with racial injustice, that had to do with equality.' I, of course, in a vacuum, don't condone violence or looting of any kind, but look back at the history of this country, and the history of revolution in this country. That's America. Protests work in America. Do you think the right to vote was just given to Black people? Do you think the right to vote was given to women? Do you think Pride Month, with everyone dancing around, having a great time, came out of nowhere? That shit came out of a police brutality riot and racial injustice riot at Stonewall. I think, unfortunately, and this is horribly sad, but this violence and this looting might be the only thing that wakes people up. Maybe you just went to peacefully protest and got shot in the face with a rubber bullet. That shouldn't have happened. That's injustice. That's an overstep and overreach by the police department. Imagine that's your life, and your whole family's life, and all your friend's lives, for multiple generations, every single day. That's the kind of random violence and destruction that we're talking about, and it's all reinforced in everything that we do in society. I hope the whole thing doesn't have to be burned down, but in the absence of anything else working, what choice have you left people? The police departments are inciting violence and the police departments are acting first, and hitting people, beating people, gassing people, macing people, and ramming them with their cars. They're running over people! I mean, you want to talk about violence? We can start there. It's horribly sad, but this is the uprising that we need. There's never been a peaceful transfer of any sort of power in this country, ever."

Michael Bennett is a multitime NFL Pro Bowler and Super Bowl champion. He also was one of the first players in 2016 to protest racial inequity and police violence during the anthem. Then in 2018 he cowrote (with me) the New York Times bestseller *Things That Make White People Uncomfortable*.

After hearing about George Floyd's murder and then seeing the subsequent national demonstrations, the feelings he experienced were "overwhelming." "What is it that makes people take life so freely?" he asks. "You feel so sad for his family. All he wanted was to talk to his mama. All he wanted was to see his family again, and still somebody wouldn't allow that. The fact is that life is given to us by God, and to see somebody take it from somebody, it's just hard to watch, especially since it was constantly shown on TV. This creates a sense of numbness. It tingles down to your fingers and tingles down into your heart and to your spine. You feel like you can't feel anything because it's just so, so deep."

Michael looked at the sheer numbers that took to the streets and saw a cry for help. "We've come so far in this world because of technology, but it hasn't solved the discomfort and the pain that we all feel, just as human beings," he said. "Technology hasn't really solved that. Things happen faster, but I think when you see everybody in the streets, it's because they feel that the American dream and the American ideology of what this country is supposed to mean to people doesn't represent them. It has never represented them in a way that they would have freedom. It's a reminder that we have so much further to go. When you think that we're flying to space, but there's still people starving, and that we're building new buildings, but there's still people with no clothes on. There are still people dying from police violence. There's still a lack of nutrition. There's still a lack of education. All these different things that are happening because of the color of somebody's skin makes you understand why people are coming out into the streets. It's because people are coming back to their senses of being connected to humanity again. Have we put income over humanity? Have we put 'things' over justice? We think about capitalism. We think about colonialism. We think about materialism. These are all the three things that we've been stuck on for a long period of time. I think we're realizing that we're really lost. We've been out of touch with the importance of the human being, and the importance of bringing people together, the importance of being united. There are so many things that divide us, but there are so many things that bring us together. I think that the racial injustice happening in this country is bringing people together in a way we haven't seen in a long time."

I asked Michael if he was taken aback by the number of athletes who were not only backing the protests but marching in the streets themselves. He said, "I think it's a little surprising, and it's not surprising at the same time. There've been athletes speaking out in the recent past, but the number of athletes is a little surprising. We've all been so attached to capitalism, and if anyone has suffered from that, it's athletes, because everything we do is from a capitalist mind-set—from how we are first treated in the NCAA. We get in there at colleges; you're already in the business. If you look at Texas football and the way that people treat high school players, there's this idea that their body is a part of this capitalism. They're almost subhuman. It breaks us and slowly takes us away from our dignity and our connection to our humanity and our people. Athletes are breaking away from that."

Then there is the question of vindication. Michael Bennett sacrificed a great deal by protesting during the anthem: he lost endorsements, he received threats, and he became a target for police, who subjected him to harassment. I asked him if he felt any sense of vindication based upon the demonstrations taking place. "Nah, I don't feel vindicated. I've been talking about this since I was a kid. The people before me have talked about it. It's the history of Emmett Till. It's the history of lynchings, the sundown towns. It's the amount of racial inequality and the racial disparities in America. The perpetual cycle of being overpoliced. The perpetual cycle of race. The perpetual cycle of being held down because of skin color. Because these issues keep happening and we have this obligation to our history and our humanity to act. We also must act because of our connection to what's happening in Palestine, the connection to indigenous people all around the world. It's the connection to humanity and the intersectionality that leaves me vindicated, because when you stand on the right side of truth, then you don't have to worry about darkness, because the light is on those issues. One who stands underneath the light is vindicated, any way it goes."

The NFL has attempted to handle this moment by saying that they believe that "Black Lives Matter" and pledging to give money to community organizations that work on racial justice issues. To that Michael said, "I think it's hard to say that you believe in these issues when we still have owners supporting Donald Trump. But I think the NFL is trying to find a common ground where they can find a balance of being a company and also being socially active. The question is whether this is about propaganda or is it about changing the lives of other human beings. I think the jury's still out on that. We think that we can throw money at it, but I think this is an issue where if you throw money at it and we don't really put our hands on the ground, then it's going to look like they didn't have the real intention of changing society. I think if you look at Roger Goodell, he has kind of missed the point and missed the opportunity. All his actions seem null and void when you look at the Colin Kaepernick situation. We're thinking, okay, if this commitment to justice is true, then why doesn't Colin Kaepernick have a job? That's an important part of the equation, but also it's an important part to help change the policy and push the culture forward."

I also asked if Michael had a message to the NFL fan base, which is overwhelmingly white. He said, "It's not just our fans. I think it's important that all people around the world attempt to understand the suffering of the many and try and really grasp the unimaginable tensions that are going to happen if we don't make change. If we intend to hide, then eventually that mask that we keep carrying around won't be enough and this social conflict that keeps coming around is going to get bigger and bigger and bigger. It's going to create something that we all don't want to have. It's important that if we don't understand the suffering and injustice of the many, then we won't have the armor of our morality. We won't have the armor of the connection of humanity. Society will fall apart because we'll be so disconnected and will be so unjust, and at the end of the day, there won't be any more peace. There won't be any more rationality, because at the end of the day, everybody's going to continue to fight. I think there's a point where we all have to stop being dishonest and come together and realize that if you break down our human DNA, our human philosophies, every human wants the same things. But at some point, we tried to create deception to act like we don't want that and create a caste system to keep us from achieving the goals that we see as fair. The Earth doesn't need us. The Earth continues to grow. The trees continue to grow. If we kill ourselves off, then that's going to be our own issue."

Given the explosion of protests, I wanted to know how people should assess him, Colin Kaepernick, and all the work they've done over the last few years. He said, "People shouldn't assess us. People should look at us as part of the whole. We're just all part of the pie, the society that I was talking about. I think there's so many truth tellers that have been on this planet before us and put all that work into telling the stories of our history. To realize that we are part of a movement is to realize that we're part of history. That's just the normal thing that everybody should be doing on the planet, being part of change.

I think that's why we're seeing so many people in the streets, because everybody is being a part of the change. We're no different. We're not special in any kind of way. We don't have any superpowers. All we have is a voice. We have a connection to human dignity and the survival of people who look like us and the survival of people who don't have a voice."

Epilogue

We Are the Positive Force

D r. John Carlos is an icon. The 1968 Olympic medalist gave us a moment for the ages when he raised his black-gloved fist to the heavens on the two-hundred-meter medal stand, alongside Tommie Smith. Silver medalist Peter Norman, standing at attention, also wore a patch in solidarity that read "Olympic Project for Human Rights." All three men paid a terrible price for daring to use their Olympic platform to speak out against racism and injustice. They were ostracized back home, unable to find work, and their families suffered as well. Yet as John Carlos said to me, "I don't regret doing it at all. The people with regrets are the ones who were there in 1968 and chose to do nothing." Today, John Carlos lives in Atlanta, Georgia, and is still active in the fight for racial justice and human rights. Given this remarkable resurgence of athlete activism, I needed to ask him for his thoughts about the current moment. Since it was the murder of George Floyd that detonated this outpouring, I asked him for his own thoughts when he saw the footage. "You're horrified to the point where you're numb," he said, "just in terms of how explicit that homicide was. I mean, there was no remorse shown, no concern for his life. Law enforcement never turned around to see, to tell their own coworker, 'Man, raise up off that man's neck!'

"It has come to this before. I spoke on this fifty-three years ago: the need to make the politicians, make the business owners, make the government, make everybody aware that this is far greater than just one individual's death. This is a humanitarian issue. People are dying all over the world needlessly, based on someone standing behind the shield."

As millions were shocked into action following this murder, athletes took to the streets and were outspoken in ways we haven't seen since 1968. They referred to people like Muhammad Ali, Tommie Smith, and of course John Carlos in claiming their place in the tradition of activist athletes and their right to be on the march. For Dr. Carlos, that took his breath away. "All these individuals, I would knock all the pictures and trophies that I have on my mantel and put them all up instead as heroes. All of the professional athletes, men, women, boys, and girls, that are taking a stance. It takes a tremendous amount of courage to stand up and say, 'Enough is enough.' I commend them. But also, I'd like to make them understand: they've been saying my name all over the country, all over the world, and that's fantastic, but I want them to study and realize that I wasn't in the moment; I was in the movement. They have to realize that they are not in the moment, in this instance; they are in the movement, whether they like it or not. This is not a one-shot deal. They have to have a clear understanding about that. Once you jump into the pool of humanitarianism, and you try and back off, you may succeed in backing off, but you're going to be seen down the line that the people have no respect for you because you didn't continue to fight."

Lastly, I needed to know if Dr. Carlos had a message for the youth: for people who are in the fight as teenagers, carrying on his name and carrying on his work. He said, "We have a great opportunity for the first time in a long time to focus on our history. Learn about who you are. Have an understanding as to who you are. Have an understanding why you're at this point now, to the point where Black consciousness is not just here in America, but worldwide. You have to understand what's going on before your time in order for you to have the ammunition, the intelligence enough to load your gun, economically, emotionally, politically, socially, to fight this cause that we're in. But you can't fight if you don't know who you are. You can't fight if you don't know your history. And if there is anything else I'd want these young people to know, it's just to make sure that they keep loving: Love thyself. Love thy neighbor. Set a precedent and let them know that we are not the negative force in society. We are the positive force."

Acknowledgments

A book usually has one, sometimes two or three, names on the cover, but make no mistake it is a collective project. Thank you so much to The New Press for taking a chance on this project. Thank you Marc Favreau, zakia henderson-brown, Maury Botton, Ellen Adler, and everyone in The New Press family. This book would also have been impossible without the great transcriber Daniel Baker, who worked with me to turn these interviews into text. Thank you to Susan Canavan and Scott Waxman, literary agents who believe in the timeless wonder of books. Thank you to Jules Boykoff for helping me make sense of all these interviews. And on the very personal tip, thank you to Michele, Sasha, and Jacob for supporting me through this endeavor and handling our family's pandemic isolation with such incredible grace. Thanks to my mom and dad, Jane Zirin and Jim Zirin. Thanks to my *Edge of Sports* pod producer David Tigabu. And thanks to my colleagues at *The Nation* magazine, particularly Katrina vanden Heuvel, D.A. Guttenplan, Peter Rothberg, and Annie Shields. Thank you to Bill Lueders and everyone at *The Progressive*. Thanks to the WPFW family, especially Katea Stitt. Thanks to my work partner of now many

\

years(!) Etan Thomas. Lastly, all the thanks go to the brave athlete-activists who took the time to speak with me and inspire the people in their communities with their courage. And lastly—for real this time—thanks to Colin Kaepernick. If you don't know why I'm thanking Colin, then start at page one and read it again. As Organized Konfusion said, "A message to the critics, get it when you rewind. . . . It's three strikes, two tokes, one time for the mind."

Index

INDEX

About the Author

DAVE ZIRIN, *The Nation*'s sports editor, is the author of ten books on the politics of sports, most recently *Jim Brown: Last Man Standing*. Named one of *Utne Reader*'s "50 Visionaries Who Are Changing Our World," Zirin is a frequent guest on ESPN, MSNBC, and *Democracy Now!* He also hosts *The Nation*'s *Edge of Sports* podcast. You can find all his work or contact him through his website, EdgeofSports.com. Follow him on Twitter @EdgeofSports.

Publishing in the Public Interest

Thank you for reading this book published by The New Press. The New Press is a nonprofit, public interest publisher. New Press books and authors play a crucial role in sparking conversations about the key political and social issues of our day.

We hope you enjoyed this book and that you will stay in touch with The New Press. Here are a few ways to stay up to date with our books, events, and the issues we cover:

- Sign up at www.thenewpress.com/subscribe to receive updates on New Press authors and issues and to be notified about local events
- Like us on Facebook: www.facebook.com/newpress books
- Follow us on Twitter: www.twitter.com/thenewpress

Please consider buying New Press books for yourself; for friends and family; or to donate to schools, libraries, community centers, prison libraries, and other organizations involved with the issues our authors write about.

The New Press is a 501(c)(3) nonprofit organization. You can also support our work with a tax-deductible gift by visiting www.thenewpress.com/donate.